INDIGENOUS AFRICAN KNOWLEDGE PRODUCTION

Food-Processing Practices among Kenyan Rural Women

NJOKI NATHANI WANE

Indigenous African Knowledge Production

Food-Processing Practices among Kenyan Rural Women

UNIVERSITY OF TORONTO PRESS
Toronto Buffalo London

© University of Toronto Press 2014
Toronto Buffalo London
www.utppublishing.com
Printed in the U.S.A.

ISBN 978-1-4426-4814-2

∞

Printed on acid-free, 100% post-consumer recycled paper with vegetable-based inks.

Library and Archives Canada Cataloguing in Publication

Wane, Njoki Nathani, author
Indigenous African knowledge production : food-processing practices among Kenyan rural women / Njoki Nathani Wane.

Includes bibliographical references and index.
ISBN 978-1-4426-4814-2 (bound)

1. Embu (African people) – Science.   2. Embu (African people) – Folklore.
3. Embu (African people) – Social life and customs.   4. Women – Kenya – Embu District – Social life and customs.   5. Food industry and trade – Kenya – Embu District.   I. Title.

DT433-545-E48W35 2014   305.48'896391067626   C2014-900132-0

University of Toronto Press acknowledges the financial support of the Government of Canada through the Canada Book Fund for its publishing activities.

University of Toronto Press acknowledges the financial assistance to its publishing program of the Canada Council for the Arts and the Ontario Arts Council.

*To Mom, Dad, Brother Anthony, Michael Lemiso,
Francis, and Murtha.
May your souls rest in peace.*

Contents

Foreword ix

Acknowledgments xiii

Map of Kenya xiv

Introduction 3

1 Food Processing: Embu Women and Indigenous Knowledges 19

2 Kenya: The Land, the People, and the Socio-political Economy 31

3 The Everyday Experiences of Embu Women 44

4 Food Preservation and Change 63

5 Gender Relations, Decision Making, and Food Preferences 72

6 Indigenous Technology and the Influence of New Innovations 79

7 Removing the Margins: Including Indigenous Women's Voices in Knowledge Production 87

8 Contesting Knowledge: Some Concluding Thoughts 98

Notes 107

References 113

Index 121

Foreword

Anyone who has visited rural communities in indigenous communities cannot escape the constant lament of their elders about the attempts of the current generation to dismiss or disempower indigenous ways of knowing as "irrelevant knowledge." The elders' defence of "indigenous" or customary ways of doing things does not imply that local peoples want to live in the past or that they are only interested in glorifying or romanticizing the past for its own sake. Rather, it is an astute realization that knowledge is cumulative. Knowledge builds on itself, and only the anti-intellectual claims that some forms of knowledge are useless, without appreciating the contexts and politics of claiming and producing such knowledge. If there is "useless" knowledge, it is defined more by the poor intent of the user of such knowledge than by the knowledge per se. For indigenous or minority scholars in the academy it is a constant struggle to legitimize their cultural ways of knowing. Today we can point to another form of intellectual politics that calls on us to subvert dominance and to shift away from Eurocentric or Western-centric theorizing and discursive practices. Personally, I see indigenous knowledge as a strategic knowledge base from which to rupture the Western academy because I am convinced that indigenous, anti-colonial analysis offers the best hope to challenge the epistemic violence of Western cultural knowledge as it relates to the material and spiritual exigencies and existence of marginalized subjects and communities. Although the insistence upon the reimagining and repositioning of difference as critical political discourse draws strength from the important work of critical theorizing, I nevertheless want to insist further upon an anti-colonial agency that enunciates itself in the talk of "border crossing" and "cultural synthesis" by inserting power into narrations about the social relations of knowledge production. So I ask, how are knowledges from the margins or periphery (that is, the South) really taken up in the "centre or core" (that is, the North)? As we note elsewhere in the critique of the political economy of knowledge production in the academy (Dei and Doyle-Wood 2006), without making such linkages and without taking into account the totalizing neocolonial impact of the processes of globalization and global capital interests we (as marginalized bodies in the North) cannot (but we must) fully understand the changing ontology of systemic violence as it impacts us at "home" when the interests of Western cultural capital feel threatened by the very same bodies "abroad" (in the South).

The field of indigenous knowledge is growing every day as critical scholarship continues to challenge the dominance of certain ways of knowing. In her thoroughly researched and well-grounded work, *Indigenous African Knowledge Production: Food-Processing Practices among Kenyan Rural Women*, Njoki Nathani Wane adds to this growing literature with a particular focus on indigenous food technologies in Kenya, and readers are exposed to the power of indigenous women's voices. We also develop a deep appreciation of the cosmo-vision of the Embu peoples of Kenya as seen through the lens of local food-processing technologies. The gendered dimensions and implications of indigenous knowledge and knowledge production in general are made clear. The desires and perils of reclaiming local cultural resource knowledge for social development are teased out. This is critical, given that scholarship about Africa still needs to respond to a key challenge: how do we capture and interrogate the local cultural resource knowledge of African peoples for their contributions to the development process?

Embedded in the food-processing technologies of Kenyan rural women are teachings on African indigenous philosophies. Women, as cultural custodians and elders, are knowledgeable about the teachings of the indigenous philosophies that highlight the society, culture, and nature interface or nexus. Very often such knowledges are discernible in the practice of everyday living or in the mundane articulations of indigenous proverbs, fables, and folktales. Education today can benefit from understanding the ways to introduce indigenous knowledges into schools and classrooms. They have much to offer in the schooling and education of youth.

While indigenous food technologies are about social economies and the relations of production, this knowledge extends to other realms of society. For example, the technologies constitute significant teachings relating to interpersonal development; self and community discipline about resource extraction and use; environmental sustainability; social responsibility; cooperation and non-violent conflict resolution; caring for others; goal setting; and responsible citizenship. Constitutive of African indigenous philosophies, local food-processing technologies teach about character development and moral values as they relate to environmental consciousness and the responsibilities of the living. As we rethink ways to transform schooling and education in contemporary contexts, it is crucial that such scholarly works on indigenous philosophies offer poignant, educative material that can allow for sustained engagement with culture, history, politics, identity, and collective agency.

More important, however, the question of knowledge, history, and identity when connected to issues of indigeneity is about a rootedness in a place and culture. Claiming indigeneity is also about spiritual healing and praxis that call for an embodiment of knowledge and culture in politicized ways. In evoking notions of the "spiritual" in the politics of claiming indigeneity, we also look for ways to deal with the despiritualization of the self and communities and to heal the disconnection between soul, mind, and body in conventional knowledge production. In many ways, the recourse to indigeneity is a struggle propelled by more than simply a desire to reclaim knowledge; it is also intended to help learners reflect on the present and to project, contest, and define. We need knowledge that provides us with new imaginings of the future, knowledge that is rooted in awareness of history but not held hostage to the past. This is well within the discursive terrain of what I have termed the politics of *epistemological equity*. Epistemological equity recognizes the multiple ways of knowing the differences in personal and collective location, subjectivity, experience, histories, and agency. In such conceptualization of epistemological equity, the question of identity, agency, and resistance assumes a new meaning beyond the claiming of a politics of reclamation of knowledge. The search for epistemological equity necessitates rescuing identity from the postmodern, post-structural rhetoric of difference and fragmentation. This is not to imply that such complicated understanding of identity is irrelevant, but I am increasingly concerned about the hegemonic readings of identity that strip the power of collective existence and politics. In other words, I am arguing that identity needs a critical social enquiry, one located in indigenized conceptions of the subject or subjectivity and agency and placed in a discursive link with knowledge production.

This will be a different conceptualization of identity – as connected, relational, and fundamentally spiritually grounded. The subject is constituted sacredly, discursively, historically, structurally, and politically. Knowledge is about making wholeness and interconnection (see also Shahjahan 2007; Alexander 2005).

George J. Sefa Dei
Department of Sociology and Equity Studies
Ontario Institute for Studies in Education, University of Toronto

Acknowledgments

There are several people without whose unyielding support this book could not have been written, and I would like to express my indebtedness and gratitude to them. I sincerely thank all the women who took time to share their personal experiences and stories with me and my research assistants. I would also like to thank the numerous people who have read different drafts of this book: Amadou, James, Paul, Mandeep, LiwLiwa, Akena, Murangiri, and the University of Toronto reviewers. Your comments and suggestions strengthened the final arguments presented. And to my family, Amadou, Koyiet, Nairesiae, Sein, Aziz, and Moodi, *asante sana*, thank you for your love.

To my Creator, thank you for your guidance at every step of the journey.

Administrative Boundary
Negele
Sudan
Kelem
Omo Wenz
Dawa Wenz
Kapoeta
Ethiopia
Dolo Odo
Lokichokio
Ramu
Kaabong
Moyale
Lodwar
North Eastern
Turkwel
Eastern
Moroto
Uganda
Marsabit
Suam
Soroti
Rift Valley
Kenya
Wajir
Somalia
Mbale
Kitale
Ewaso Ng'iro
Tororo
Western
Mado Gashi
Nzoia
Eldoret
Butere
Kakamega
Isiolo
Bilis Qooqaani
Nyahururu Falls
Nanyuki
Kisumu
Tana
Nakuru
Kericho
Garissa
Lake Victoria
Nyeri
Embu
Nyanza
Central
Kindaruma dams
Mara
Thika
Narok
Musoma
Nairobi
Nairobi Area
Eastern
Athi
Magadi
Pate Island
Garsen
Lamu
Coast
Mount Kilimanjaro
Tsavo
Galana
Malindi
Arusha
Voi
Moshi
Indian Ocean
Numba ya Munga dam
Mombasa
Tanzania
Pangani
Pemba Island
Tanga

INDIGENOUS AFRICAN KNOWLEDGE PRODUCTION

Food-Processing Practices among Kenyan Rural Women

Introduction

Indigenous African Knowledge Production is a product of research conducted among Embu rural women in Kenya between 1993 and 1995. Although the research was conducted almost twenty years ago, very little has changed, as demonstrated in my other research projects (2006, 2007, and 2010–13) and yearly visits to Embu. In all, 200 female subsistence farmers were selected, of whom 177 agreed to participate in the research. Of those, 123 filled out a questionnaire. Seventy-seven of the 123 were also interviewed, during which 14 shared their life histories. No specific systematic method was employed in selecting the participants, because my intent was to visit a homestead and request a life history or an interview or the time to fill out a questionnaire. In-depth interviews form the core of the book's analysis, and the completed questionnaires provide the statistical data; however, the focus was on information gathered during the interviews. Several factors were explored in considerable detail and comprised each woman's daily routine; frequently eaten foods and the process of their preparation; serving patterns; the decision-making process; property ownership and division of labour; and attitudes towards indigenous technologies, specifically regarding relations between indigenous processing technologies and new technologies.

Kenya is a country of startling contrasts and striking diversity. With Ethiopia to its north, Somalia to the east, Tanzania to the south, Uganda to the west, and the Sudan to its northwest, Kenya is a crossroads between East Africa and the Indian Ocean. Its northern and eastern regions occupy a high plateau where rainfall is sporadic and the land is dry. Further south, the land sprouts shrubs and grasslands. In the southwestern highlands, part of the Great Rift Valley – a chain of lakes, valleys, and volcanoes, including Mount Kilimanjaro – carves a magnificent swathe that ultimately runs across much of Eastern Africa. In addition, it is in Kenya, amid escarpments and scattered lakes, that one finds evidence of our earliest ancestors (see Salim and Janmohamed 1989).

I was born in this land and came of age within traditions enriched by more than a thousand years of cultural exchange among the peoples of the Nilotic, Bantu, Hamitic, and Cushitic language groups, whose lives were shaped by the fertility of the land or the lack of it. Agriculture was foremost in the survival of those whose ethnicity and type of food production were related and marked by subsistence strategies that exist to this day. The percipience acquired over many centuries from countless generations of varied peoples who lived and continue to live on this land reflects a deep respect for the environment that, along with the cultural crossover between major ethnic groups, formed the foundations of an evolving indigenous knowledge. The knowledge encompassed not only agricultural practices and methods but also the social and the spiritual. In their observation of the natural world and the vagaries of the landscape these peoples nurtured a healthy respect for the land and all living creatures on it, growing food crops for domestic sustenance and often for trade. Maintaining this ability was integral to indigenous practices, and food-processing techniques have been passed down through the centuries in the understandings of women who today engage in agricultural practices in much the same way as did their forebears. Their domestic food-processing techniques are part of a wider indigenous knowledge base that regrettably is under threat, a threat that was first precipitated by colonization and then by the onrush to embrace globalization and technological advancements. Political, economic, and social mores have changed and are still changing, but there are aspects of the indigenous knowledge of Kenya, as well as that of other African countries, that continue to motivate and sustain diverse ethnic cultures. Mandala, describing the history of food preparation in Malawi, states that women were central to this process because their lives were organized around food processing. Mandala goes on to note that historians have ignored this in addition to all the other activities related to the process. The author notes that it is women who have shown more willingness than have men to embrace new food-processing technologies such as mechanical grinding mills because they reduce the time spent in food preparation (Mandala 2005, ch. 7). Athough there are personal benefits to adopting some of these new techniques, the women do not like the fact that they have to travel long distances to reach a machine for grinding corn (Mandala 2005). Also, they then have to wait for their turn and pay for the corn to be grinded. In my study among the Embu women, although some welcomed the new technologies, many felt that poverty prevented them from embracing them. Both overtly and covertly, there has been a disruption of the indigenous ways of knowing, learning, and teaching for most of the world's indigenous peoples. Indigenous educators often lack the understanding of how and when such knowledge should be reproduced, and many custodians depreciate their own indigenous knowledge.

This latter aspect was glaringly obvious during my interviews with Embu Kenyan women, who were surprised that I had journeyed from Canada to learn from *them*. As one exclaimed, "What could you learn from me, an old woman with no education? I cannot speak English. What do I know except how to hold my digging stick, how to tell when it is time to harvest my crop, how to pick the right herbs to cure diseases, or how to prepare my indigenous foods? I am sure you have not come all this way to learn about *that*!" But I had, setting out with a purpose that for me was inevitable. These were my people, the bearers of all that I am, the embodied reflections of my spirit. My time in the West could not change that. And the invisible thread that linked us should not be broken because I had acquired a Western education. I would not and could not allow such a travesty. That old woman, the custodian of ancestral knowledge and history, is in a wider sense an educator, although such an idea might not occur to her. Her knowledge is substantial and crucial to the food-processing practices that sustain her family. Her education is eminently a practical and valid example of its marginalization from Western classrooms and Western mores.

I had returned to Kenya with the express purpose of gleaning a greater knowledge and understanding of Embu women's food-processing practices. Within Embu culture one can walk to a homestead without prior notice, a practice that I followed during my fieldwork. My familiarity with the culture helped me to interpret the situations in which I was not welcome, and in such instances I quickly retreated. If the initial greeting welcomed me, I made myself comfortable and gave no indication of being in a hurry. I did not launch into my reason for being there until we had exchanged news about ourselves, families, cows, goats, crops, rain, politics, and more, which often took an hour. For a non-Embu person who is accustomed to getting down to the business at hand as quickly as possible, this approach could be misinterpreted as time wasting and unnecessary, but for the Embu community it was polite and crucial. It was a respectful exchange of thoughts, ideas, and background, which is necessary to the Embu in getting to know the person, the *being* that crossed the homestead threshold, and, of course, letting the person know *them*. Only then did I begin the interview process. In addition to information gathered through personal and group interviews, secondary material and official documents were reviewed to provide additional background.

The purpose of writing this book is not only to bring attention to salient aspects of indigenous culture but also to bring particular attention to indigenous food-processing techniques. The process allowed me to reflect on my education in Kenya and the way I had shown unflinching loyalty to everything I learned in the Western-inspired classroom (Wane 2003a). In fact, my parents encouraged me to acquire these Western knowledges to enable me to lead a supposedly "better" life. I do not fault them. They, I realize, saw the writing on the wall and knew that as the world changes, so must I. They left it to my heart to retain the indigenous knowledges I had already assimilated and apply them where and when necessary. I attended missionary schools from grades five to twelve with a high sense of hope and self-improvement. Guided by European missionary nuns who used the British curricula, I was persuaded and compelled to memorize material written by Western scholars, an inevitable requirement to pass British-set examinations. My local knowledges, values, and world views were not tolerated in the colonial classroom. Expectedly, I took great pride in reading and reciting the works of Shakespeare, D.H. Lawrence, George Bernard Shaw, Hemingway, and Dickens and regarded those who did not read or enjoy reading these books as backward and intellectually illiterate. In all honesty, I viewed African writers who agitated for inclusion of local knowledges, languages, and world views into the curricula as troublesome scholars (Wane 2003a, 321).[1]

Respect for all that had sustained my young, pre-colonial mind eroded under the "light" of colonial discourse. My conviction and my conversion were almost absolute. It never occurred to me that with my colonial indoctrination and education I was ignorant of the myriad factors surrounding colonization and its insidious effects on my own mind. However, it is important to note that reverting back to indigenous knowledge per se would be an illusion. Many people of African ancestry do not have a homogenous indigenous knowledge. In addition, my indigenous knowledge systems and traditions have been subjected to different forms of colonialism, neocolonialism, and distortion. Again, our cultural resource knowledge is not frozen in time and space. A discussion therefore of indigenous knowledge in relation to food-processing practices is complex, and my intention in this book is to write the stories of Embu women in relation to their role in contributing to knowledge production.

Of all the aspects of Western colonial mechanisms, the one that Africans found most seductive was formal Western education. In acquiring literacy in English or French, we quickly realized that a university education opened the door to economic advancement, individual attainment, and a new-found dignity that ultimately provided the keys to political power and self-government or self-advancement. Anti-racist educator and scholar George Dei confirmed, from the responses of participants in his research in Ghana, that many Ghanaian students acknowledged and adored the cultural asset that colonial education brought to individuals, and they therefore rejected educational reform (current or future) that would put at risk the Western system of knowing (Dei 2004). Indeed, from an economic standpoint, the actions of my parents have paid off as the acquisition of colonial education has enabled me to travel to Europe and North America in order to further my education. However, I do so now with heightened awareness and greater wisdom. My mind is not merely a repository to be filled with Eurocentric world views but is capable of interrogating those world views and discarding ideas that represent psychological bondage for me as an African woman.

Let me be clear, however, that a Western education is not necessarily to be rejected out of hand. It serves a purpose. It empowers individuals. It opens the wider world to minds willing to stretch beyond ethnic, cultural, and geographical borders. But the privileges often come with a great price: loss of local culture, values, knowledges, and the many traditions once held dear during upbringing in a rural community (Smith 1999).[2] Such was my own experience. As did African scholar Malidoma Somé, I have realized that vibrant aspects of my life were taken away from me during the years spent acquiring a colonial education (Somé 1994). The colonial institution assumed that its goal was my goal, and for a long period this indeed was the case. The result was a slow submersion of my identity and everything that I once respected and was familiar with as an African woman.

It is not surprising that I saw myself as a stranger in my own land of birth. The geographical domain of my village, however, is still familiar, and I still speak my local language. Yet, I see that my ways of doing and thinking had been disproportionately skewed towards the West. I have had to confront this dichotomy of my own life: an Embu by birth and a Westerner by education. During my conversations with my research respondents I recognized that their deep knowledge of the ecology, nutrition, and indigenous technologies exceeded that of most government planners and officials and of what I had gained through several years of Western education. Even though many of these indigenous women were proud of my achievements, it was I who looked at *them* with envy. They have what I have lost. My identity has been compromised, but my journey towards reclamation has begun.

I realized that I could resolve my internal dilemmas if I could debunk Western-formulated myths and help rescue from almost certain obscurity the indigenous knowledge of Kenyan women about food production. It is a significant aspiration because by so doing I will be able to pass on this knowledge, help prevent the slaying of another cultural way of knowing, and protect this birthright for future generations. The hope is that, through this book, these women and other Kenyans will be encouraged to appreciate their precious food-processing knowledge. Embu women confirmed that they have been forced to depend on commercially prepared herbs, packaged foods, and motor-driven maize mills. Any change introduced to a society has some benefits, but its reliance destroys self-sufficiency, contributes to dependency, and affects the assurance, self-identity, and self-direction of community-controlled survival. It is no small matter.

I am aware of my indigenous limitation as a woman assuming the responsibility of speaking for my elders without appropriate authority. However, I am aware that tradition can bestow on me the power to play the role of a cultural linguist who carries and refines the words of elders for public consumption and understanding. With this in mind, one should not read my role in this work as that of an educated, middle-class woman who believes that subaltern women cannot speak for themselves. I am but a facilitator, using my greater cultural and linguistic access to rupture and subvert the sense of comfort and complacency that colonial educators have in knowledge production, validation, and distribution.

I do not romanticize the way of life for Kenyan rural women, because there is no romance in survival, only necessity. I hope to draw attention to what is lost in knowledge research when vast areas of indigenous living are discarded in the name of advancement. It is also hoped that the awareness of policymakers will be raised concerning the unique and precious gains that a country might derive if local knowledges were used in food preservation. My arguments are not centred on the premise that these knowledges should not be interrogated by other knowledges. I endorse an approach in which various knowledges interrogate one another to arrive at a solid consensus that is relevant for human growth and development.

Chapter Overview

Unlike recent works involving African women as objects or artefacts of sociological and cultural studies, this book attempts to move beyond geological, archaeological, and anthropological analytical frameworks towards an anti-colonial methodology. The study supports the voices of African women as participatory agents of change and critically examines how these women make sense of the construction and sustainment of the textual imaging of their experiences. In so doing, it moves away from "othering" and appropriates their voices in an effort to represent indigenous knowledges in an academic context that honours African women. Embu women's food-processing technologies can be documented without reproducing the epistemic violence that has so often accompanied documentary research practices.

It is critical that indigenous women's technological knowledge be situated within a world view that is shaped by collective understanding and interpretations of their social, physical, and spiritual world. The legacy of colonialism, which discredited indigenous knowledges, is the creation of a gap between two worlds of knowledge production, the Western and the "other" – in this particular case, African. To view Western-based educational systems as the producers and inheritors of the only authentic epistemology is to do violence to the objective validity of other epistemologies. While some ignore and disparage indigenous ways of knowing, others continue to conserve them. With formal education and its inherent rewards occupying the pedestal of success, indigenous knowledges have become devalued in the very minds and hearts of the Embu women themselves. Ironically perhaps, my own formal education and research have drawn me closer to my indigeneity. I came to realize the importance of self-reflection to moving beyond post-colonial indoctrination. Many times during my research I found myself as both an outsider and an insider. I was a researcher, and an outsider when the participants spoke from their location as rural women; at the same time, I was an insider because I occupied a shared location with them. During previous visits to the village I had often experienced a sense of alienation, and many times I felt that I had lost the rural connections of my early years and that now I belonged to two worlds and could claim total acceptance in neither. For instance, during an encounter with one of the participants she was quick to point out that I was a foreigner (in my own village), yet I was one of their children. Thus, for reasons that are embedded in colonialism, the long-established division between the West and the "other" re-emerged during my encounter with most participants. Up to that moment, I had not encountered, on an experiential level, an awareness of the divide that had been created between me, a Western-educated woman, and my rural upbringing.

In order to advance beyond attempts to decentralize the objectification of the "other," we must focus less on critiquing the totalizing forms of Western historicism – although it is necessary to understand and evaluate their impact – and more on engaging in a discourse of possibility in which indigenous women's voices and knowledges can be heard, appreciated, and cherished. Such a discourse will enable us to move beyond the need to correct distorted images of African sustainability, drought, starvation, and disease, and engage in not merely *citing* what is wrong but *repairing* the damage. It will also reveal the intricate roles that various members of the household play because, as Mbilinyi (1997, 335) states, "most peasant households rely for their subsistence or reproduction on a combination of economic activities, many of which are not organized within the household or under the control of the household head. Household subsistence depends increasingly on separate activities of wives, husbands, children and other household members who retain individual control of the proceeds for many of those activities."

This move towards an anti-colonial methodology and framework for understanding African women and indigenous knowledges will transform existing approaches to knowledge production. The knowledge and world views of millions of the world's indigenous peoples are shaped by their relationships with their environments. This is crucial for their survival because the knowledge gained builds their cognitive understanding and interpretations of their physical as well as their social and spiritual worlds. Their lives are enriched by observation and interpretation, which form the foundations of their wisdom. Indigenous knowledge is learned through direct personal experience, not abstractions; it is holistic, non-linear, qualitative, and intuitive. Instead of comprising explicit hypotheses, theories, and laws, indigenous knowledge is made up of a cumulative and collective knowledge that is continuously interpreted. It tries to understand systems as a whole and not as isolated, interacting parts (Nyamnjoh 2004). Scholars have used various working definitions of indigenous knowledges, with many agreeing that the notion of indigenousness can originate from local consciousness and long-term occupancy of a place. This translates into unique indigenous knowledge that comprises discernment and skills developed outside a formal educational system of thought, and that is embedded in the culture of a given location or society.

Although indigenous peoples cannot claim monopoly over indigenous knowledges, the issue of authentic indigenous identity should not be glossed over in discussions (Wane 2005). Some indigenous scholars note that while "outsiders" may, for example, know the names of indigenous herbs used to preserve food or prevent insects from destroying crops, and even understand how they are applied, this does not necessarily make the outsiders indigenous. Battiste and Henderson (2000) and Malidoma Somé (1994) argue that there are differences between having knowledge of indigenous herbs and knowing how their various properties can be used as a curative or a preventative for people, animals, and plants. They have, therefore, concluded that the potency of using local herbs, preservatives, and others – concurrently with ritual songs, chants, prayers, and other ceremonial practices – is more efficacious. To learn about indigenous perspectives requires alternate research methods, and input from elders is essential. Sustaining indigenous knowledges demands a willingness to put what is learned into daily practice. For instance, it was not unusual for the women I interviewed to hesitate to answer my questions or allow me to accompany them in their farms or observe their preservation rituals. Many times I had to convince them that I was a keen learner and not just a researcher who wanted to collect data for purposes of academic advancement.

Indigenous knowledges are not homogeneous. According to Dei (1994), the normative claims made of African knowledge systems do not indicate that other indigenous or aboriginal communities cannot share similar knowledges. Universally, indigenous knowledges share the following characteristics: the acknowledgment of and belief in unseen powers in the ecosystem; the contention that all things in the ecosystem are interdependent; personal relationships that reinforce the bond between persons, communities, and ecosystems; the responsibility of those holding such knowledges to pass them on; and a genesis within respective communities. In addition, they are culturally specific, holistic, oral in form, and not documented or systematic. Most of the indigenous experiences of the Embu rural women reflect a oneness with the spirit of the land, the people, and Embu cultural beliefs. Indigenous knowledges go to the heart, spirit, mind, and subsequent practices of a community, reflecting symbiotic relationships, with no demarcation between various aspects of the women's lives.

When the subject of African indigenous knowledge is raised, it is often necessary to define the term. To the African, this knowledge is not linear, and its essence is shared by communities whose world views engage and embrace the totality of *being* and living (Dei and Asgharzadeh 2001; Thiong'o 2005; Wane 2003b). It is this commonality that allows Africans to understand one another's culture, politics, and economics. As African indigenous knowledges are dynamic and founded on diverse life experiences, a neatly packaged definition is elusive. In this book I have used the terms *indigenous* and *traditional* interchangeably.

Each of the chapters will explore the salient aspects of indigenous knowledges that Embu women hold, as well as focusing on the indigenous food-processing techniques that they have employed since time immemorial. The first chapter introduces the Embu women with whom I embarked on this incredible journey, and I explore their indigenous knowledge of food production and the main teachings that I acquired from each woman. In chapter 2, I provide an overview of the landscape of Kenya, its land, and the role of women in the protection of it; the people and the roles and customs of each family and community member in the cycle of food production; and the socio-political economy, in which I examine the impact of colonialism on Kenyan society and its economy. In this chapter I reflect on the changes (if any) that have taken place in the fifteen years since my research was conducted. I also provide the current political situation as we await the inauguration of President-Elect Uhuru Kenyatta, the son of Kenya's first president, Mzee Jomo Kenyatta. Chapter 3 explores the everyday experiences of Embu women as well as the marginalization they experience at the hands of their male counterparts. Not only do I detail the impact that patriarchy has had on them, but also I highlight the significant role and abundance of knowledge that they carry for their family and community. In chapter 4, I look at the methods of food preservation employed by Embu women, as well as the changes to indigenous storage systems that have evolved as a result of technological change. Chapter 5 examines gender role, decision making, and food preference. In chapter 6, I explore indigenous technology and the influence of new innovations. Particular attention is paid to what women are doing in relation to indigenous knowledge. Chapter 7 examines what it means to include indigenous women's voices in knowledge production and how it is that certain voices are included or excluded in knowledge production. In line with African feminist methodology, I place women at the centre of my analysis. The last chapter provides some concluding remarks in terms of indigenous knowledge.

African Feminism: Situating Ourselves within an Anti-colonial Framework

This study employs an African feminist theoretical discourse as an anti-colonial prism through which to counter an oppositional discourse. African feminism did not develop in the academic setting but in the villages where the inclusion of women was evident in the social, economic, ritual, and political spheres (Steady 1989, 5–8). The nature of African village life was one of collectivity, not autonomy. By virtue of the collectivity, African feminism developed through the bonds that women had with other women. This meant that African feminism emerged as a unified collective thought. When African women were oppressed by slavery and colonialism, they were forced to develop techniques that ensured their survival. Struggling against oppression was not a singularly individualistic task; rather, these women used their collective framework for support (Steady 1989, 20–1). I invoke *colonialism* within the context not of something foreign or alien but of anything imposing (Dei and Asgharzadesh 2001). This implies that colonialism did not originate from indigenous peoples' encounter with the West and therefore did not end after political independence in Africa. Rather, colonialism has always existed among indigenous people prior to the Western colonial encounter. Indeed, stories and experiences of patriarchal domination and its impacts on local women have been recorded in many scholarly works about Africa (see Adjei 2007; Aidoo 1965; Dei et al. 2000; Dobson 1954). Such encounters, as enunciated in the cited works, clearly attest to the reality that colonialism is an ongoing condition for many African indigenous communities even in this "postcolonial era." The roots of African feminism therefore are found in the features of most African societies that stress the ideology of communal, rather than individual, values and the preservation of the community as a whole. However, during colonialism a drastic change occurred in African societies and, in particular, the lives of African women.

Establishing and achieving a framework for this change must take into account African feminism, which has been defined in various ways. Filomina Chiomia Steady views African feminism as an epistemology that enables African women to theorize their gendered status in society, and examines how they continue to be exploited and marginalized under the expansion of capitalist states (Steady 1989). Nnaemeka (1997) sees it as an ideology that evokes the power of African women and their identities amid obstacles, causing them to critically analyse themselves as subjects of oppression and victims of gendered labour subordination. Ogundipe-Leslie (1994) emphasizes that what African women do and how they do it provides the framework for their gender-centred awareness. Buchi Emecheta articulates her position on this subject: "I am a feminist with a small 'f.' I write about the little happenings of everyday life. Being a woman, and African born, I see things through an African woman's eyes. I chronicle the little happenings in the lives of the African women I know. I did not know that by doing so I was going to be called a feminist. But if I am now a feminist, then I am an African feminist with a small 'f'" (Emecheta 1988). Emecheta further argues that *womanism*, more than the term *feminism*, captures the complex, nuanced, and multiplicity of African women's experience. To be fair to Emecheta, she was not suggesting that *feminism* is the wrong term to be used in Africa. The truth is that African women's experience, within the context of gender relations, is very complex and likely to be misunderstood when read within the Western construction of feminism. As Nfah-Abennyah states, "most feminists differentiate sex from gender. Sex is understood as a person's biological maleness or femaleness." Maleness or femaleness brings up a differentiation that does not necessarily amount to one being more important than the other. The differentiation, however, goes with a responsibility.

Using the traditions and customs of indigenous Africa to guide and understand gender role in Africa is important. After all, Joy James (1993) informs us that to choose to live outside our traditions, apart from our ancestors and people, means losing the roles of living thinkers, servants to the spirits, community activists, and, the deepest realities they reflect. Among the Embu culture, responsibility is accorded more attention than are rights. The Embu believe in each individual contributing her or his quota to the welfare of the family, the community, and the society as a whole. Roles played by individuals are only acknowledged if they lead to the collective good of the family, the community, and the society. For example, the role of a mother is considered as a gift with which the Creator has endowed women, and no matter how "caring" a man is, he cannot play this role in the same way as a mother can. Thus, it does not seem out of the ordinary in Africa for women to be expected to keep home by cooking food, providing a comfortable environment and a healthy (tidy) shelter, and caring for the children and the husband. The man also has the role of "tilling the ground" to find food and provide various amenities for the family. It should be noted that while the parents go on with their responsibilities, the children play their part by running errands and helping with the home chores. These different roles complement one another to keep the family and the larger society going in Africa.

In fact, disharmony and chaos are created when one party fails to perform its roles in these unwritten gender and age arrangements. For example, a man can easily be accused of infidelity when he refuses to eat his wife's food and prefers to eat somewhere else, especially when his wife is available to cook for the house; it can be a legitimate ground for demanding divorce. Ontologically, it is predicated among indigenous Africans that food and sex are the two major routes to a man's heart; therefore, a man who eats another woman's food has inadvertently expressed interest in that woman. Of course, this gender arrangement can easily be misinterpreted as patriarchal domination in Africa if it is read through the lens of Western feminism. However, Embu women would disagree completely with such conclusion. This is not to suggest that patriarchal domination does not exist in Embu and in Africa as a whole. In fact, it exists, and African women do not hide their disapproval about this patriarchal arrangement. However, what constitutes patriarchy may be slightly different in Africa than in the West. For instance, in North America the financial arrangement in which bills and daily expenses are jointly paid by spouses is an accepted practice. Similar practice is frowned upon in Africa. Even in cases where women earn more than their men, it is still the responsibility of the men to provide for their household. In many cases African women have supported their men with additional funds, especially if they are not earning enough, but this role of support must not be mistaken as one that usurps the financial obligations of the men. An African man who cannot take care of his household is often mocked by the community members as having lost his "mojo" (what really makes him the man of the house).

It is within this context that Emecheta advocated for a new terminology that could easily capture the experiences of African women. The Western brand of feminism would be incomplete and inadequate to capture African women's experiences. African women activists and writers are astutely aware of advocating for a feminism that speaks to the specific realities and locations of African women and placing them at the centre of analysis. The politics of privilege and power – especially the power of self-definition and self-determination – are fundamental to African women's liberation and empowerment. As it is crucial to highlight the specifics of African feminist consciousness, so it is important to note that this theory also espouses the importance of women challenging each other by being self-reflective, acknowledging our privileges, and recognizing the situations in which we oppress others who do not possess similar advantages.

Aidoo provides further insightful thoughts and analyses to this long-standing gendered consciousness of many African women: "The women's movement has definitely reinforced one's conviction about the need for us to push in whatever way we can for the development of women. But I don't think that one woke up one morning and found that they were talking about the development of women, and one should also join the bandwagon – no. What it has done is that it has actually confirmed one's belief and one's conviction. Our people say that if you take up a drum to beat and nobody joins, then you just become a fool. The women's movement has helped in that it is like other people taking up the drum and beating along with you" (Aidoo 1998). Aidoo's African-centred analogy demystifies the fallacy of feminism or womanism as a Western or borrowed ideology. In order to place African women's gendered consciousness at the centre, Aidoo deploys women's drumming as a powerful metaphor. The drumming represents the gendered knowledges that African women possessed prior to and during the emergence of Western feminism and the women's movement as it is conceptualized today. The women's movement and other forms of feminism have joined the cause, drumming a message that African women have known for some time. Aidoo shows the complexities of African feminist theory and the distinct ways that different African women, depending on their location and experiences, conceptualize African feminism. However, the majority of African women are not preoccupied with articulating their feminism of gendered consciousnesses; they simply act on it (Nnaemeka 1997). According to Nfah-Abbenyi (1997, 10), "African women struggling both on behalf of themselves and on behalf of the wider community are very much a part of our heritage. It is not new and I really refuse to be told I am learning feminism from abroad ... Africa has produced a much more concrete tradition of strong women fighters than most other societies. So when we say that we are refusing to be overlooked, we are only acting today as daughters and granddaughters of women who always refused to keep quiet. We haven't learned this from anybody abroad." As custodians of African culture, values, traditions, moral standards, and knowledges, African women's education occurred within the context of strong oral traditions and customs. Folk tales, narratives, fables, mythology, songs, riddles, and proverbs are passed down to the next generation through the spoken word, rather than through a written text. This is fundamental to understanding how African women's gendered awareness is theorized and practised.

Some African women claim that feminism is not an African ideology and that what is labelled today as African feminism was adopted by African women educated in the Western tradition. They reject feminism because they feel that it aligns them with white, middle-class, Western feminists (see Nnaemeka 1997). Others also dismiss African feminism because they perceive it as an imported ideology that has the potential to damage good African women (see Nnaemeka 1997). For yet others, the rejection of feminism is predicated on the assumption that it had existed in Africa long before *feminism* became a watchword in the West. Those in favour of this last point are quick to point to historical figures who pursued social justice, such as Nana Yaa Asantewaa, the queen mother of Ejisu of Ghana, who led the war against the British in 1901 (see Nnaemeka 1997).

Although they may not have used the term *feminism*, African women have a long history of gendered consciousness (Ogundipe-Leslie 1994). However, in order to clearly establish the intrinsic nature of the problems faced by those wanting to retain, elevate, and disseminate the indigenous knowledges of African women, it is critical that we examine these knowledges. Only then can we begin the process of understanding and preservation. I also take an indigenous theoretical framework as a starting point to my African feminist discourse. African feminism is part and parcel of African women's way of knowing. This fusion was quite common to the women with whom I talked during my research in Kenya. In their discussion they stated quite clearly that their concerns for community took into account their male counterparts as well. Situating African feminist theory in indigenous knowledge provides a starting point in critical elaboration of the consciousness of what one really is – a product of the historical process to date – which deposits in each an infinity and does not leave an inventory. I therefore employ

African indigenous knowledge to assist me in the process of compiling an inventory that could be used for rethinking a revitalized and renewed African feminism as anti-colonial thought.

In conclusion, this introduction has provided the reason that I undertook this work, the theoretical framework that I have employed, and a brief overview of the chapters. Thus, at a highly personal level, this book is intended to be not only a step towards embracing indigenous identity but also a tribute to indigenous African grandmothers, mothers, and daughters by acknowledging the essentiality of their role in producing and sustaining indigenous knowledges and practices. In addition, I would like to build on the work of other scholars who have examined the role of women in community activities (such as craft industries) and economic activities, which, as Zeleza has stated, tend to be ignored by researchers: "One of them is the processing of staple food and beverages both for domestic consumption and for sale outside the household. Domestic food preparation was of course a daily chore, mainly undertaken by women. It involved pounding and grinding grain, peeling and preparing tubers, fetching water and firewood, as well as cooking itself" (Zeleza 1993, 210). The following chapter introduces the Embu women who shared their wealth of knowledge on indigenous ways of food processing.

1 Food Processing: Embu Women and Indigenous Knowledges

My experiences of witnessing and participating in the processing and consumption of organically grown, indigenously prepared foods made me understand a multinational company's reason for appropriating the imagery of rural women's food-processing activities. However, that imagery cannot capture the *rhythm* of these women in their food preparation, and the concomitant teachings. During my research I was riveted by their activities. The women were seated on short, home-made stools, surrounded by everything necessary for their work. I never witnessed a single moment when their hands were idle. With rapid movements they would reach for the firewood that was drying by the heat of a fire in a *rutara* (raised platform), take water from an earthen pot at their side, and dip utensils in an urn to soak. "A wide variety of food-preservation techniques were used during the nineteenth century. For example, meat, fish and vegetables could be preserved through drying, smoking, and salting. The Khoikhoi, for instance, used to hang meat up to dry after it had been lightly salted. The meat could be eaten without further preparation. This practice was widely adopted by the European settlers, and the meat came to be called biltong" (Zeleza 1997, 2010; Elphick and Shell 1989; Delegorgue 1990). Although the research I conducted was very extensive, for this book I have chosen to focus on the voices of fourteen Embu women and the knowledge they imparted to me. The following brief descriptions give some insight into the lives and the wisdom of each of the regal Embu women who are the custodians of traditions such as food processing that once gave their communities a power and a sense of oneness with each other and the world around them.

Cucu

Cucu (meaning "grandmother") was more than eighty years old at the time of our interview. (Later, in 2003, I visited her home again and was informed that she had passed away.) She lived in a one-room house, which was adequate for her purposes. The "kitchen" area was near the door, and it was there that I spent many hours with her, listening to her story. The room had a three-stone fireplace, a low-level bed made from twigs, a big earthen pot filled with water, a grinding stone, a mortar, and two small cooking pots filled with herbs. A raised platform served as a place for storing harvested produce and for drying firewood. Cucu explained that everything she needed was in that room. The kitchen's strategic location enabled her to keep an eye on what was happening outside and to call when necessary. I witnessed Cucu prepare harvested grains for storage, cook her meals, and mix different herbs for curing colds, fevers, and stomach ailments. Cucu explained that she had acquired her knowledge through observation, trial and error, and imitation and from folklore, stories, and proverbs. Her participation in the study enriched the discussion and knowledge acquired in the research. Cucu brought rich cultural knowledge and experience to the articulation of issues. Although she was humble in her presentation of ideas, it was obvious that she spoke from a particular cultural and experiential prospective that granted her a discursive integrity over the issue of indigenous food processing and storage. Cucu was a great addition to the research.

Wachiuma

Wachiuma, a seventy-year-old woman, taught me the importance of using the appropriate technology for food processing and preservation, thereby reminding me that one's culture is central to oneself. She sees the importance of orality in knowledge transmission: "It was through songs, proverbs, idioms, storytelling that we learnt our traditions, acquired knowledges of our clans and our ancestors. It was always fascinating to watch and listen to songs, wise sayings of women at work. My grandmother always used to say to me, '*Mwana wi kio ndaturag gia kuria*' (a hard-working child can never miss what to eat or sustain its life)." Orality carries not only the message but also the feelings, spirit, and emotion of the speaker. For many people like Wachiuma, orality is power. Indigenous women have long recognized the power of the spoken word in knowledge production. Cruikshank has argued against the notion of treating spoken words as objects to be collected and stored for archival purposes. Like Rosaldo, Cruikshank has suggested that orality should be treated as text in knowledge production (Cruikshank 1992).

In another observation, one that relates to new technology, Wachiuma raised questions about the use of stoves powered by solar energy as a reliable alternative to the use of local sources of fire: "This is a box standing up, and at the top the fire comes out. How would I warm my legs? How can you use a standing box for cooking? How would I roast my yams, sweet potatoes? The fire [pointing to the three-stone fireplace] keeps me warm. When my grandchildren come to visit me, they sit there or where you are seated [pointing to the unoccupied side of the fire]. They tell me about school, and I tell them stories about our clan, our culture. Everything happens around the fire."

Wachiuma raises many issues connected with new technologies that are borrowed wholesale from the West without any consideration of the local situation. Within indigenous knowledge, the kitchen is not simply a place for cooking but also a site for producing and sharing knowledges. Therefore, the settings and the type of technologies used in the kitchen should be able to facilitate the transfer of those knowledges. In addition, the absence of heating systems within local communities implies that indigenous Embu women have to rely on fire as a source of heat to keep them warm. In fact, it is the warmth of the fire that makes the kitchen a gathering place, a space that allows the sharing of indigenous knowledges through its many forms of transmission. It also becomes the environment in which to impart moral lessons and discipline to the young ones. Unfortunately, the new stove was introduced without taking into consideration the local sentiments, culture, and traditions. Not surprisingly, local Embu women rejected it. Such resistance to changes in technologies was based not on the ignorance or foolhardiness of the local women but on the unsuitability of the product for local use.

Another aspect of the new stove that makes it less appealing to Embu women is the fact that it is not designed to facilitate the use of local utensils and cooking pots, which are made of aluminum or clay. It then becomes obvious that using the stove requires changes not only from firewood to stove but also from the commonly used local utensils to those employed in the West. The change in the cooking utensils also implies that certain local foods – particularly those that require considerable energy and time to prepare – must be put aside because the new tools and stove do not make their preparation easier. The negative ramifications of these situations push the women to resist the introduction of such technology.

Kanini

Kanini, a sixty-five-year-old participant, was very eloquent in describing the use of her cooking utensils, which were given to her by her parents when she got married:

> My cooking pots have served me well for many years. My parents gave me the *cuvurias* [aluminum pots] and the *gitararu* [an indigenous winnowing tray made of twigs that is smeared occasionally with cow dung to give it a long life and to ensure that it can hold grains; it is a very special gift given to all newly-weds by their mother], and my mother-in-law bought the earthen pot for me. Why should I abandon them? I value these pots [touching them]. My children have bought me new pots, but they never last for more than a year. But these pots have been part of us since I was newly married ... I will pass them on to my grandchildren ... Do you see that earthen pot? It was baked especially for me. Why would I give it up when the pots we buy in the market cannot keep my water cool? ... No, I will not be persuaded to abandon any of these items so that I can embrace change. I am from the old and I will always be that way.[1]

The voice of resistance as shown in the narrative of Kanini calls for a forum of educators, researchers, and developers to examine the possibilities of including local knowledge in our thinking and to question our predilection for change. People like Kanini, because their world is not included in the so-called global village, refuse to adopt its new technologies. Yet, this refusal, as viewed by Western discourse, is considered evidence of ignorance or primitivism. I have argued that indigenous Embu women are concerned not only about the technologies that increase yield in food production but also about those that can support holistic sustainability of ecological systems. If technological advances are unable to sustain these systems, rural people will continue to resist them.[2]

Ciarunji

Ciarunji, is seventy-six years old and agrees that new technologies are efficient but come at a price. She sees the connection between indigenous technology and womanhood. "When you use a grinding stone, you are in harmony with nature. You are attentive to what you feed your family. When you buy food from the shops, something is lost in the process." She feels that in the latter case she cannot identify with the process of adding value to the food. When she talks of the disadvantages of using a tractor, she explains: "Women are connected to the land through their reproductive cycle. When a woman agrees to have a tractor plough her land, she gives up the handling of the soil to something foreign. The machines will uproot any plants, interfere with soil composition, and, least of all, not experience the sacredness of nature. The women's digging sticks, though time consuming, ensure proper mixing of the topsoil and the manure. As the women prepare the land, they 'talk' and question what causes variations in soil structure or reasons for a poor harvest."

Ciarunji's comments evoke the spiritual connection that these women have with the land. She sees the using of one's hands to work the land as a means of becoming one with its sacredness. The land, therefore, is not abused for capital gain and is seen not simply as a source of wealth but also as a force of life; it is sacred, it belongs to the ancestors, and it will punish custodians who misuse it. Indigenous women see their actions as accountable to the ancestors and refuse to harm the land upon which their survival depends. According to Ciarunji, the use of a tractor may be efficient and time saving, but it detaches women from the land and its crops.

> The maize mill, the tractors, the maize shellers make work easier ... but you need money to use a maize mill. If you want your *shamba* [family plot] to be ploughed, you have to pay for the service ... you lose something. You see, when you use a grinding stone to make your flour, there is some connection between you and the food you are preparing. When you use a maize mill, you lose something to the machine. Again, when you use a tractor, you cease to know your land. As for the packaged flours or maize, it means you are eating what you do not know, and it is important that you know what you are eating ... or what you are feeding your family with. You lose sense of your products when they were harvested, how they were cared for, etc.

Rwamba

Rwamba is sixty years old and shares Ciarunji's concerns. She believes that the all too eager reliance on new technology by the younger generation, without consideration of the possible repercussions, should be a major concern. For Rwamba, although the use of new technology can make work easier, its negative consequences cannot be easily dismissed. The use of tractors and maize mills can create environmental pollution and even harm humans in the long term: "The maize mill and the tractor produce noise that is bad for your ears, and the smoke from the machine is not good for your lungs." We see that the main concern for these women is the effect of the new technology on nature and the environment, rather than the personal benefits they would gain from its use. Their views are inseparable from their spirituality.

Miller sees spirituality as something that transcends the consciousness of the self and personhood and that lies in the social values connecting the individual to the group, community, the Earth, and the entire cosmos (Miller 1999). Furthermore, Dei has argued that spirituality and questions of ecology go hand in hand. "Knowing about one's lands is to acquire knowledge about the spiritual and material connections between society, culture, and nature. African spirituality connects the physical with the metaphysical world" (Dei 2004). According to Bishop, our spiritual ways of knowing should teach us that there are beings other than humans because there is "a somatic acknowledgement of our connectedness with and commitment to our surroundings, human and non-human" (Bishop 1998). It is this spiritual understanding that persuades these rural Embu women to look beyond the short-term advantages of new technology to the long-term deleterious effects of environmental pollution. They see their obligation as one of protecting the land and the environment for those who will come seven generations after them (Goodleaf 1993). All too often our thirst and desire for personal fame and wealth blindfold our conscience and prevent us from looking beyond our short-term comfort. Not surprisingly, researchers embark on explorations that they know could be ultimately harmful to society. Developers overlook damages and desecration wrought on sacred places, all in the name of profits. As citizens of Western society, in our search for individual rights, we can sometimes ignore collective societal responsibilities. Today, uncontrollable destruction of the ozone layer, extinction of endangered species, and senseless pollution of water have created an environmental time bomb of monumental proportions. We seem to have ignored the repercussions of our actions, leaving the solution of these problems to future generations.

Mama

Mama is sixty-six years old and enjoys preparing home-made porridge. She explains that by using their hands the women can tell the quality of the porridge. They put their hands in the mixture and, after removing them, ascertain from the residue on their hands whether there is a need to add more paste or to grind the residue at the bottom of the mixture. Mama also says that from the time she wakes in the morning she tells the time by interpreting the size of the shadows of the trees. The shadows inform a mother when it is time for her to go to the farm, when the children will return from school, and when she should go home to feed them.

Indigenous knowledges evolve according to need and are developed and modified for efficiency. They accumulate and represent generations of experiences, careful observations, and trial and error. The community builds on these knowledges, expands them, and refines them out of necessity and out of a spiritual resonance with its environment. Children watch their mothers at work and try to imitate them during play. When allowed, they carry out tasks under the watchful guidance of their mothers or aunts. Mastery is gradual, and the learning processes in daily activity, training, and education are not relegated to specific times and places. Older participants in my research were unwilling to compromise their indigenous knowledges because the very essence of these knowledges lies within the community collective and everyday activity. They are a unifying force that brings nature, people, ancestors, and spirits together for the common good. Mama still remembers making the local brew using indigenous technology, the freedom with which it was made, and the women and men who gave their time without question or hesitation:

> The women spent a whole day grating sugar cane, and the men squeezing juice out of the grated cane ... Even when the sugar-cane hand-drive mill came, the men and women would still work together. The women would ferry the sugar cane to the mill, feed the mill while the men would drive

it. Later, the women would use a cloth to sieve the brew ... Come to think of it, now that you remind me, when the motor-driven sugar-cane mill was introduced, all this togetherness disappeared. People started brewing their own brew secretly, while others stopped brewing it altogether, because you had to have the money to pay for the mill.

One can deduce from Mama's response that the introduction of new technology has inspired an increase in individualism, unnecessary competition, and an inclination to promote the interests of a few over those of the community. As Shiva (2000) noted in a different context, the introduction of motor-driven sugar-cane mills disrupted the web and tissue of society. Laws were instituted to prohibit people from making their own beer. According to the chiefs, these laws were meant to bring order to beer production and protect the owners of the mills, who had invested substantial amounts of money in milling technology. People abandoned lifelong practices because of the fear of being arrested. Some young women think that the new technology provides alternatives while others believe that it creates dependency.

Njura

Njura is thirty-one years old and the mother of three children. She has a high-school diploma (one of the few women with any form of Western education), and she enjoys weighing the pros and cons of the indigenous ways of food processing and preservation. When I met her, she was working at a tea-drying factory, making approximately two Canadian dollars a day, and in our conversation she was quick to make this observation: "Although these machines make our work easier, we become lazy and dependent ... When you get used to making *ugali* [corn meal] from the maize flour made by these machines, you start disliking the hand-ground flour, and then when you have no money, you could starve ... it has its good points and bad points." Njura was very keen to talk about her experiences of tea-picking practices and preparing indigenous teas for her family. In addition, she did note the complexities involved when technologies are introduced and that the change has an impact on consumption patterns. Njura's observation has been noted by Hansen (1992) on cook stoves and charcoal braziers in Zambia.

Angelina

Angelina is fifty-eight years old. She talked a lot about her husband and the rules that he had established in the home. From my conversation with her it was clear that Embu society is patriarchal as well as patrilineal. Although the women play integral roles, the father is the head of the family and in charge of the homestead. "The head" of the family, in the Embu context, is synonymous with ownership. This was confirmed when Danieli, Angelina's husband, stated, "My wife knows everything in this homestead is mine, everything!" Angelina agreed, saying, "It is true what Danieli has said about owning everything. When I came to this home, I did not bring anything. This is his home, and everything here is his." Another husband, Lemani, said, "I own everything here – women, children, the cows, goats, and even the fleas belong to me. Nobody can touch anything in this homestead without consulting me first." Angelina further stated: "Everything is ours, but of course he is the man of the house, and I guess that makes him the owner ... I guess my role is to look after the property for the benefit of all." Angelina's statements reveal acceptance and submission. She sees herself not in the centre but on the periphery, playing the role of caretaker. Yet, it would be incorrect to assume that there are no women who are assertive and make independent decisions. Rwamba stated, "What would my husband tell me about the homestead, about food?" She is questioning her husband's authority by focusing on what she knows best, the food.

Alice

Alice is thirty-five years old and has no children. Although quite prosperous compared to the rest of the community, she did not look happy. She was living in a semi-permanent house (a house built using mud bricks and grass; its structure is designed to withstand cyclones and to account for winds and the smoke produced by fire) with two of her nieces who had been given to her by her sisters to look after until she got her own child. She expressed her fear of remaining childless: "I do not know why I do not get pregnant. It is not the same when you do not have children. People treat you differently ... Until you have a child, people think you are a man. I hope I will get a baby soon, otherwise my husband may decide to take me back to my parents."

There are social differences in Embu society that may on the surface seem strange or unthinkable in Western society. Yet, Westerners often react in similar ways to women who choose a career over parenthood or who fail to give birth. It was in the West that the description of a wife as being "barefoot, pregnant, and in the kitchen" originated. Western feminism was, in some measure, a response to this patriarchal attitude.

Wawira

Wawira (meaning "hard-working woman") is forty years old and married, with four children. She had a grade-seven education and wanted to go to high school, but she did not meet the required passing mark. Her family's annual income is less than seven hundred and twenty Canadian dollars.

Kanyiva

Kanyiva (meaning "petite") is twenty-seven years old and married, with four children. She lived in a semi-permanent house, and her household had an annual income of ninety Canadian dollars. She repeatedly narrated her busy life and said she did not like anything to do with indigenous food-processing practices. She had a grade-eight education.

Wangeci

Wangeci (meaning "opportunity") is twenty-six years of age and is a single mother with one child. She lived in a semi-permanent house in her parents' compound. She earned her living by selling vegetables, and her annual income was one hundred and fifty Canadian dollars. She always preserved her food with indigenous herbs and was happy to do so.

Waithera

Waithera (meaning "one who is always clean"), at twenty-four years of age, was the youngest participant in my research. She had one child and was expecting her second. In my conversation with her, it was clear that she had different views about indigenous technologies. She had little or no knowledge of them and therefore had to depend on her family for assistance in matters relating to indigenous knowledge. She did not want her friends to know that her family relied on indigenous knowledges, thinking that they would probably laugh at her. Waithera's role in the research was important because it helped me to understand what appeared to be a generational shift away from the existing interest in and passion about indigenous knowledges.

What is so different from Waithera on one side and Kanyiwa and Wangeci on the other side? What makes Waithera ashamed to admit that she has interest in indigenous knowledges, while Kanyiwa and Wangeci openly embrace them? Is Waithera's attitude a general reflection of her generation or an exception? Given the posturing of Waithera, is there a future for indigenous knowledges among the Embu community in Kenya? Waithera's, Kanyiwa's, and Wangeci's participation opens up a discussion about these questions.

Marigu

Marigu (meaning "one who stores food for the next season") is twenty years of age and is married with two children. She did not complete high school but hoped to join adult literacy classes when her children were older. Marigu's household made less than two hundred and forty Canadian dollars a year from the sale of farm produce. She did all the farm work alone because her husband lived in the city and came to visit once or twice a year. She wanted to join her husband in Nairobi (the capital), but he was unemployed.

The fourteen women introduced in this chapter provide the necessary data to show that underneath Embu women's food-processing and production activities are forms of indigenous thoughts and local knowledge systems that have an enduring African epistemic identity. Most of the older women know the origin of their home-made cookware and are repositories of other indigenous technologies. Ciarunji, for example, knows that the pots and pans came with people from the neighbouring district of Mbere who used them as barter for food. Mama stated that her grinding stone was collected near the riverbed and was then worked on by her husband. As for the mortar and pestle, Mama mentioned that every man in the homestead used to know how to make them. In the "old days" men made tools and utensils for their women. However, except for the grinding stone, most tools can now be bought from the shops. The older women think that the men have lost the skills to make these tools owing to the acquisition of formal education. For this reason they have challenged formal education and insist that the educated among us have contributed to the destruction of the environment and the erosion of indigenous knowledges. They also insist that although indigenous technology is tiring and time consuming, it is "free."

The women's sense of producing indigenous knowledges raises salient issues for those who think that knowledge should be accepted as legitimate only if it is acquired through empirical research. It is the practice of learning through careful observation that informs the local lesson that "wisdom comes with age." It is believed that an adult's observations concerning nature enable them to discern and offer suggestions that pertain to various circumstances and situations. The next chapter describes the country in which these women live (Kenya), its people, and the socio-political economy, as well as the participants' views.

2 Kenya: The Land, the People, and the Socio-political Economy

Kenya can best be understood in terms of the links connecting its land, people, and socio-political economy. It is a nation of forty-three million people (2012 census) and fifty-two ethnic groups that fall mainly into three linguistic categories: Bantu, Cushitic, and Nilotic. The largest of these groups is the Bantu, to which the Embu community belongs. Some 85 per cent of Kenya's population live in rural areas, with most concentrated in the fertile southern half of the country. The annual population growth rate of 2.4 per cent (Kenya National Bureau of Statistics 2010) is among the highest in the world.

The Land

The country's food production has failed to keep pace with its dramatic population growth (Kiteme 1992). The problems resulting from this growth are reflected in a broad spectrum of environmental impacts. Intensified farming practices have led to overfarming, and an escalated gathering of wood for fuel has led to soil erosion, deforestation, and desertification. The impact on natural resources and the land is alarming. The food situation is Kenya has been made worse by numerous droughts, which have caused extreme damage to food security. These droughts have left major challenges not only for the Embu women but for the government. In the last fifteen years the government has been constantly asking other countries for aid so that Kenya can provide enough food for her population. Environmental degradation causes draft, and many women who were interviewed in this study made frequent reference to it, as shown below.

Most of the women interviewed lamented the changes that had brought about environmental degradation over the years. Cucu expressed her sentiment: "*Gaka* [grandchild], so much has changed ... so much has been destroyed, and there is so much that is foreign that you should be the one telling me why we never get enough rain, and if we do, so much of it pours and takes away the little [land] that was left ... You are the one who has gone to school. How can we explain all this?" (Nathani 1996; interview with Cucu, 1993). Although Cucu had not heard about the depletion of the ozone layer and was not aware of the way in which fertilizers can interfere with soil composition and structure, she was nonetheless able to read the signs. Her question, "How can we explain all this?" raises a legitimate concern about the acts of omission and commission that have fostered the environmental problems affecting rural communities. Cucu had witnessed the destruction of virgin forests, the building of projects on top of graveyards, and the felling of sacred trees that resulted in the elimination of indigenous ceremonial grounds. For her, these were signs of disrespect for both the community and Mother Earth. Younger advocates of development might well argue that Embu women, such as Cucu, are resistant to change. Yet it is clear that despite their lack of formal education the Embu women are capable of looking at issues both logically and philosophically. Cucu pointed out that whenever a forest is cleared for the construction of a road, whenever large tracts of land are cleared for planting, and whenever a hydroelectric station is built to provide electricity to urban populations, poor rural families suffer profoundly from the social and economic imbalances. Moreover, the clearing of forests, shrubs, and bushes not only eradicates natural resources but also interferes with the natural life cycle and support systems on which many depend. Cucu further states: "By the time you are my age, the world will be completely destroyed ... Look around you. Where are the thick forests that we used to have? ... Kirimiri was thick, and the canopy created by the trees would not allow the rays of the sun through ... These days, people have cultivated up to the top of the mountain. Man's greed has chased the spirits of our ancestors that used to live there ... For us this was a sacred mountain ... but its sacredness has been destroyed. *Gaka* ... your generation needs to halt or slow the pace of destruction" (interview 1993).

Indigenous society has always acknowledged women's ecological knowledge. Looking back to indigenous society, Cucu compared her time growing up in rural Kenya with what is happening today:

During my time ... if the rains failed one season, we offered sacrifices to Mwene Nyaga [Creator] and we received rains ... Your generation waits for handouts and foods from *ng'ambo* [overseas] ... I can still remember like it was yesterday when women made sacrifice for rains. It was a solemn occasion for women ... A child like you could not take part in this ceremony. This was done by women who had stopped giving birth, also [those] who had not had their monthly period for several moons. This ceremony took place under the Mugumo [fig, Ficus thonningii] tree. The sacrifice consisted of black or brown goats, which came from all the clans, and honey beer. The slaughtered goats and honey beer were placed in small calabashes which the women held with outstretched hands. In unison, they would repeat the following words seven times – "Mwene Nyaga, these are your things, take them and give us ours" – after which the women placed these calabashes and the honey beer under the tree and, walking backwards, would leave the sacred grounds. Soon after, the rains came. Mwene Nyaga always listened to our cry ... but these days, things have changed. Our people have polluted everywhere; Mugumo trees have been cut down. We have no respect for anything. During our time, there was control, the tradition, the customs and belief system governed us. We were obedient and treated everything around us with care ... our trees, the soil, our animals, and people.

Cucu, with an exquisite and straightforward simplicity, speaks of a situation that should be at the forefront of all Earth Summit meetings. Her words expose the continuing, worldwide desecration of our environments. The women's sacrifices to Mwene Nyaga, the Creator, reveal their awareness of the essential reciprocity between humans and nature and reflect a reverence for taking from nature as well as giving back to nature. Cucu's analysis of the destruction of the Earth was grounded in practical knowledge acquired through her long relationship with the land and her indigenous customs and beliefs. These women's survival is now threatened because the land that sustained them has been degraded, and nature's reproductive cycle has been interrupted. However, the women I interviewed made it clear that they were not categorically opposed to what the new changes had to offer; they were only against the destructive element that was embedded in the development paradigm. Rwamba puts it best: "I am not against new technology or new foods or the new learning. What I am opposed to is the total rejection of the past without understanding what the past has to offer your generation ... We should learn from you, and you should also be ready to listen to us."

The People: Roles and Customs

Among the Embu the man is respected and obeyed by all family members. Traditionally he is addressed as "*Baba* (father) of (so-and-so)," but never by name. The woman is accorded similar respect in terms of address and is referred to as "*Mama* of (so-and-so)." A woman who chooses to have a career over children is deemed a social misfit. A woman who remains childless within this society is an outcast and considered a "man in woman's clothes." She can never be referred to as Mama of so-and-so, and her husband is always teased and laughed at. Embu family is circular rather than linear, and this is readily seen in the practice of naming children. Each woman seeks to "replace" the four grandparents, beginning with the names of the paternal grandparents. If the first child is a boy, he is named after his paternal grandfather; if the second child is a girl, she is named after her paternal grandmother. If the second child is a son, he is named after the father of the wife, and so on. After the four grandparents are "reborn," subsequent children are named after the parents' siblings. A woman will continue giving birth until all the parents are "born." If the woman gives birth to girls only, then she has to continue trying for a boy, and vice versa. As a result, families tend to be very large – all in search of the right sex to name the parents. Some ethnic groups in Kenya name their children according to the time of the day, the day of the week, the condition of that day, the state of the woman when she was expecting the child – such as active, lazy, generous – or the season during which the child was born. The failure to bear a male child could cause a woman to be divorced, because if a man dies without a male child, his name will be discontinued as soon as his daughters marry. This could be seen as one of the factors behind the polygamous and large families in Kenya. The practice of divorcing a woman because she cannot give birth to a male child is slowly dying out, especially among the elite. However, it has become a common practice among educated men and women to accept a polygamous family set. It is not unusual for an educated man to have more than one wife. In the early 1980s a man would be embarrassed to mention his second wife, but today it is more acceptable. This is an area where more research could be conducted.

Embu communities comprise a number of homesteads, most of which are situated adjacent to their family's field. A hedge or a wire fence with a single entrance encloses some homesteads, while others are set in open space. The number of buildings in each homestead depends on the make-up of the family (monogamous or polygamous), the age and sex of the children, and the presence of unmarried relatives and grandparents. A monogamous homestead with young children might have only two or three structures – the family house, a granary, and a latrine. A polygamous homestead will have as many houses as there are wives. A homestead that has adult children as well as grandparents will have additional houses because the boys sleep in separate quarters away from their parents, and the grandparents have their own houses. If there are single daughters with children, or married sons, in a home, they too will have their own houses. Ideally, then, the homestead has housing for the paternal head of the family, his wife or wives, their unmarried children, often his married sons, and occasionally unmarried male or female relatives. Until recently the male head of the homestead lived separately in his own *thingira* (a man's house), and on either side of this house, in a semicircular formation, would be the houses of wives, children, and grandparents. Next to these houses are the granaries for each wife, and at the rear is a pit latrine (Davidson 1987).

In most of the homesteads that were visited during the research for this study the houses faced an open compound or *nja* where many family activities such as food processing, feeding, playing with children, and receiving visitors took place. It was also in this space that most of the interviews were conducted. During the dry season the head of the family makes a fire in the evening, and the men of the home usually sit and pass time while waiting for the food to be prepared.[1]

Today the many homesteads that were constructed either from mud, which was plastered with cow dung mixed with ashes and sometimes white clay, or from timber, which was thatched with grass or corrugated iron sheets, have been replaced with permanent structures. During the interviews in the 1990s many women expressed a preference for iron roofs, stone walls, and concrete floors, which would reduce their yearly responsibility for repairs. This preference has been attained as the young working adults have built better homes for their aging parents. Families that live in semi-permanent houses are few and far between. Many houses have metal gutters attached to iron sheets to gather rainwater and thereby reduce the constant task of fetching water from a river, stream, or well. What is important to note is the permanence of a separate house (round in style, and grass thatched) used for cooking purposes.[2] All the homes still have pit latrines and lack showering facilities because family members bathe in a nearby river. Sixty per cent of the respondents had lived in the same location for more than twenty years.

The construction of semi-permanent houses is a joint effort between men and women. The men put up the structure, and the women cut and bring home the thatching grass, do the roofing, smear the walls and floors with mud, and later plaster them both with a mixture of cow dung and ashes. With permanent houses, however, the men do all the construction. Traditionally, the site on which the house was to be built required a ceremony. Ciarunji, a participant, recalled the practice from her youth: "The grounds where the new house had to be built had to be sprinkled with a small amount of beer. This was done to call for the ancestral spirits and seek their help in the construction of the new house. Unfortunately, this is no longer the practice" (interview 1993).

We can see that many transformations have taken place in which indigenous ways have been supplanted by today's technological advancements. Sustainability of the land has undergone drastic and adverse changes, some indigenous customs have been eroded, and Kenya's socio-political economy has been affected by a number of factors.

The Socio-political Economy

The political economy of Kenya is similar to that of other African countries, reflecting a colonial legacy characterized by underdevelopment and external dependency. However, despite a fragile political economy, Kenya enjoyed tremendous growth during the first decade of political independence (1963–73) (Kenya Development Plan 1994–9; 2000–4). Between 1964 and 1987 the gross domestic product (GDP) increased from £330.10 million to £5,702.54 million. However, despite this increase, the economic growth was not sustained, particularly during the second half of the 1970s. Among the economic reasons for this reversal were the global oil price increases during 1973–4 and 1979–80, the deteriorating terms of trade for primary commodity exports, the fluctuations in exchange rates, a rise in interest rates, and the world recessions of 1975–6 and 1980–2. Internally, the droughts of 1974–5, 1980–2, and 1992–6 also contributed towards the stunting of Kenya's economic growth (Kenya Development Plan 2005–9, 2010–15; Mburugy and Ojany 1989).

In recent years, according to the World Bank, Kenya has been upwardly mobile in terms of economic growth. In 2011, GDP was 4.4 per cent, and the projection for 2012 was slightly lower at 4.3 per cent in anticipation of an economic slowdown during the election year. The World Bank's report (2012) indicated that the country's economy had stabilized and that Kenya needed to create more jobs for its burgeoning population of educated youth. Johannes Zutt, World Bank Country Director for Kenya, noted that the ratio of Kenyans engaged in farming activities had declined to less than two-thirds of the workforce. This situation is reflected among the Embu population: there are fewer youth living in Embu now compared to the 1990s when I carried out my research; most of the young people have migrated to the cities in search of jobs.

It is interesting to note that the inequitable income distribution and an ever-widening gap between the rich and the poor have become worse since the 1990s. The 2012 World Bank report noted that the government has not managed to find a solution to the rising income gap, the rising unemployment, and the poverty. In this vein, Sen (1985) has observed that development projects are often indifferent to the interests and needs of the poor, while Ikara (1989) goes further, arguing that such inequities pose a real danger to internal security.

Other issues also dominate the spotlight on Kenya. Not only have its economic policies come under scrutiny, but it is evident that the place of women in Kenyan society has undergone significant deterioration. Since the completion of my research in the mid-1990s, however, and in the last decade Kenya has made great advances in the political arena. Although studies by Nzomo (1993) and House-Midamba (1990) show an increasing marginalization of Kenyan women, the new constitution provides for women representatives in Parliament. For instance, when Parliament resumes sometime this year, 2013, there will be at least forty-seven women representing their counties. From 2002 to 2012 there were eighteen to twenty-two women in the Kenyan parliament, out of 224 members; sixteen of the women were elected, and six were appointed by the president.

In the entire civil service only 9 per cent of senior positions are held by women. Owing to discriminatory practices those who do occupy decision-making posts make few inroads and, in most cases, are silenced if they try to go against the mainstream. Indeed, such women come to be perceived by their colleagues as "men" because by venturing into traditionally male domains they are seen as having lost their femininity.

Although there are myriad examples of the state's gender discrimination regarding property ownership, inheritance, marriage, divorce, rape, and wife abuse, women in positions of authority have neither debated nor lobbied for change. Their silence suggests that they fear their own victimization or removal from office. Alternately, it might be assumed that they are essentially in agreement with their political colleagues. However, in 2007 a domestic violence bill that had been introduced by Njoki Ndungu, a nominated Member of Parliament, was passed after lengthy debate. Many women are sceptical about its effectiveness and are waiting to see whether it will be put into practice. It is evident that Kenyan women, for their own empowerment, need to develop strategies that do not depend primarily on the benevolence of men but depend on what they can do for themselves by banding together and aligning themselves in partnership with gender-sensitive men.

Nzomo (1987) has suggested several strategies for helping women to form a united and empowered front: first, creating structural links between urban and rural women; second, raising awareness among both sexes regarding gender issues; and third, encouraging women to write their stories that describe their contributions to social, economic, and political development as well as the distinguished acts they performed during Kenya's struggle for political independence. Muthoni Likimani had already carried out the third strategy. In 1985 she wrote an inspiring account of the heroic efforts of women, including her own, during the fight for independence. She highlights the women's organizational skills and how they handled responsibility under extreme circumstances, including torture, humiliation, and the threat of death, while remaining ever loyal to their cause.

The Impact of Colonialism on Kenya and Its People

To understand its full impact on Kenya and, specifically, on Embu women, it is useful to review the events in Europe that took place prior to colonialism. According to Sen (1985) and Mies (1986), during the Industrial Revolution in Europe the family became the centre of consumption, and production moved to the factory. The propertied classes forced their women out of productive cottage industries and into housewifery, while lower-class women and their children became a reservoir of cheap and exploitable labour. Moreover, as the main concern of capitalists was to maximize production and profit, little attention was paid to the conditions under which these lower-class women and children worked. Both Marx (1997) and Engels (1973) observed that the worst conditions for women and children were found in the factories.

For the ruling classes, control over women's labour and reproduction became increasingly significant, and complex systems of male domination on the one hand and female subordination on the other emerged to support their exploitation (Mbilinyi 1994). For example, the championing of such concepts as "male prowess" and "the weaker sex," respectively, provided ideological justifications for oppression (Ahlberg 1991). As the colonizers imposed capitalism and imperialism beyond Europe, they brought into the subjugated territories these concepts, including Victorian attitudes towards women – that they be modest, genteel, and submissive to men and be excluded from having a public voice. When brought to Africa by European colonizers, such attitudes served to erode the social status of African women. This diminished social status has survived for generations.

In the pre-colonial era, African women occupied central roles in the national economy and their social status was secure. Recent gender studies corroborate that gender relations in pre-colonial societies tended to be more equitable and just compared to those of the present-day and that women (at least, elderly women) held power and had control over basic resources (see Ahlberg 1991 and the Kenya Development Plan 1989–93). Women's power and control began to decline after the imposition of a colonial ideology of production for the extraction of profits, which supported the class system existing in Europe.

Ironically, the view of the colonialists prevails that African women benefited in innumerable ways from their "emancipation" from the "bondage" of tradition. It has been widely argued that literacy, which typically is characterized as a positive transforming tool,[3] continues to be highly beneficial to African women. Yet it was through the promotion of literacy that colonizers were able to override the existing local cultures. Interestingly, during the early phase of colonialism girls were denied access to education, and when they were eventually allowed to attend school, the education system was used as a major tool for socializing them to assume domestic roles.[4] Western-style education played two major and essentially negative roles in indigenous women's lives. First, the indigenous customs and values that hitherto had supported the social system were dismantled, and, second, women lost equal access to ownership and control over basic resources and were relegated to a disadvantaged position that has persisted to the present day.

The introduction of Western capitalism via colonialism disassembled African socio-economic systems and generated unequal and dependent social, political, and gender relationships.[5] The profound psychological imprinting of colonial structures on both the individual and the national psyche of Kenyan society has yet to be fully assessed.[6]

Despite their losses, Embu women have much to offer society. Their precious food-processing knowledge is a crucial component of their wisdom. It is only fair to recognize that Kenya has been working towards the restoration of women to their active roles in not only the development of the economy but also ownership and control of the wealth derived from production. As measured by education, health, urbanization, employment, and income, the quality of life of women has indeed improved since independence. However, as much as these are laudable gains, they fall well short of embracing true and equal gender partnerships across social, political, and economic spectrums. It appears that the biggest obstacle for rural Kenyan women continues to be the social, economic, or cultural systems.

Within this tortuous equation one cannot ignore the effect of structural adjustment programs (SAPs) on Kenyan women. Scholars such as Mbilinyi et al. noted the contradictory claims that have been made concerning the impact of SAPs on various nations and gender relations. They argue that while countries such as Ghana and Tanzania have made remarkable economic recoveries, others have experienced economic deterioration, and the outcome of such programs has generally been retrenchment, privatization, cost sharing, and devaluation. This, in turn, has led to a higher cost of living, lower incomes, a decline in public social services, and growing insecurity for the majority.

In addition, a documentary on SAPs, *To Be a Woman* (Kipusi and Riid 1992), indicates that the programs have not been favourable to women. Feminist writers such as Nzomo, Idemudia, Stamp, and Shiva assert that SAPs are structured on patriarchal guidelines and depend on patriarchal social relations to support the adjustment process at household, community, national, and global levels. In their view, the SAPs reinforce rather than challenge existing patriarchal structures.

Since the SAP initiative, women and other disempowered groups have participated less than ever before in the decision making surrounding macroeconomic policies. A male bias has been retained in development policies, leading to the devaluation of basic human needs, especially regarding reproduction.[7] The reduction of government and donor support for social services has increased the workload that women carry in the home and community. It has strengthened the gender division of labour in the household and reduced women's access to regular formal employment and earning power. Lower household incomes have forced women and girls to work harder, and they have been relegated to the household tasks of collecting firewood and water, processing, and cooking. Without such work on the part of the women, communities and even the entire economy would collapse. Another negative aspect of the SAPs has been the lessening of the time available for women to carry out these tasks as well as care for children. In short, the emphasis that SAPs place on production and market principles has increased the dichotomy between production and reproduction and has strengthened the gender division of labour, thereby reducing women's access to basic resources, such as improved technology and social services.[8]

There can be little doubt that the SAPs implemented in Kenya have affected the role of Embu rural women and their indigenous food-processing technologies. Slightly over 50 per cent of the Kenyan population is female, and of that number approximately 88 per cent live in rural areas. These women are responsible for 80 per cent of the farming activities and perform 90 per cent of the family and household chores and 40 per cent of the livestock care. In addition, a quarter of the wives are de facto heads of households owing to either the death of their spouses or their prolonged absences as they search for work in urban areas.

Statistics reveal that most women are married by age twenty-four and that the average number of children born to such women is six. As a result, most rural women are caught in an endless cycle of pregnancy, birth, childcare, farm work, and household duties.[9]

The Kenyan government has spoken repeatedly about its commitment to issues facing women, most notably since the historic Year of Women in 1985. However, more than a quarter-century after its initial promise, the government has yet to move beyond rhetoric and initiate significant improvements in the living standards of rural Kenyan women. Many households survive on less than four hundred American dollars annually.[10] Issues surrounding gender and women's marginalization in state politics, families, workplaces, or schools rarely become the focus of public discussion. Whereas the roles of women as homemakers, child-bearers, and caretakers were valued in the past, today they are undervalued in urban, capitalist Kenya.

The implementation of SAPs brought untold suffering to the poor, particularly to women and children who have had to bear the heaviest burden of the current economic crisis. While the vulnerable position of women has been recognized by the World Bank and has resulted in programs to address female poverty, the effectiveness of these programs is undermined by a male dominant ideology that serves to maintain women's marginalization rather than correct the existing structures.[11] Historically, neither the World Bank nor the International Monetary Fund (IMF) has shown sufficient recognition of the power inequities between men and women as a developmental problem. Although both organizations emphasize the importance of mobilizing women for social change, they have not taken into account the well-documented fact that women have greater capacities – endurance, perseverance, and ingenuity – for coping with crises than do men (Kenya, Republic of, 1992).

African women have had to deal with multiple issues including many or most of the sociological effects of change. According to Nzomo, women have always been at the receiving end of family crises, and she notes, "The totality of these effects means it is women who suffer the greatest psychological stress created by the hardships of impoverishment and inadequate services due to their roles as providers and caretakers of the children, the elderly and the sick" (Nzomo 1993, 19). What still remains to be addressed, therefore, are strategies to ensure that women are able to participate actively in the design of the policies and packages that will alleviate their own poverty. This position was supported in the Abuja Declaration on Participatory Government. Addressing the role of women in Africa in the 1990s, the declaration states that all government and non-governmental organizations "should involve women in the design and implementation of development programs so as to make them more active and effective participants in economic, social, political and cultural change" (Blake 1993, 10). However, the declaration also observes, "Several studies on women in development suggest that the conditions of women have worsened. That is, they are poorer, live in increasingly hazardous environments, and have lost the supportive mechanisms of the past" (10). The declaration exemplifies how easy it is for governments to make fine-sounding pronouncements, but how common it is for them to fail to implement them. Blake argues that this is the most significant and frustrating element in the development problematic of the way in which to integrate human resources for overall societal development. Women simply have not been seen as part and parcel of this problematic, despite the elaborate lip services that have been paid to the notion of "women in development" (Blake 1993, 2).

For all their vaunted potential, SAPs have resulted in an erosion of both the quality and the quantity of those things that once met women's needs. For example, the risk of women dying from pregnancy and various causes related to childbirth has not decreased but increased, and it is currently estimated that 700 maternal deaths occur for every 100,000 live births.

The negative effects of the current social, political, and economic policies on Kenyan women are conspicuous and alarming; the impact of SAPs on Kenyan women is no different than that on women in other Third World countries. In all cases, women's quality of life has become more arduous during periods of so-called adjustment.

3 The Everyday Experiences of Embu Women

In her book *Counting for Nothing,* Marilyn Waring queried elements of the United Nations' System of National Accounts (UNSNA), noting that the indices used in the system consciously negated the positive contributions of women in domestic chores. She used a daily itinerary of four women (three of which follow) to buttress her concerns.

> Consider Tendai, a young girl in the Lowveld in Zimbabwe. Her day starts at 4 a.m. when, to fetch water, she carries a thirty-litre tin to a borehole about eleven kilometres from her home. She walks barefoot and is home by 9 a.m. She eats a little and proceeds to fetch firewood until midday. She cleans the utensils from the family. After lunch and the cleaning of the dishes, she wanders in the hot sun until early evening, fetching wild vegetables for supper before making the evening trip for water. Her day ends at 9 p.m. after she has prepared supper and put her younger brother and sisters to sleep. [Yet] Tendai is considered unproductive, unoccupied and economically inactive. According to the international economic system, Tendai does not work and is not part of the labour force.
>
> Cathy, a young middle-class North American housewife, spends her days preparing food, setting the table, serving meals, clearing food and dishes from the table, washing dishes, dressing her children, disciplining children, taking the children to daycare or to school, disposing of garbage, dusting, gathering clothes for washing, doing the laundry, going to the gas station and the supermarket, repairing household items, ironing, keeping an eye on or playing with the children, making beds, paying bills, caring for pets and plants, putting away toys, books and clothes, sewing or mending or knitting, talking with door to-door salespeople, answering the telephone, vacuuming, sweeping and washing floors, cutting the grass,

weeding, and shoveling snow, cleaning the bathroom and the kitchen, and putting her children to bed. [Yet] Cathy has to face the fact that she fills her time in a totally unproductive manner. She, too, is economically inactive, and economists record her as unoccupied.

Ben is a highly trained member of the U.S. military. His regular duty is to descend to an underground facility where he waits with a colleague, for hours at a time, for an order to fire a nuclear missile. So skilled and effective is Ben that if his colleague were to attempt to subvert an order to fire, Ben would, if all else failed, be expected to kill him to ensure a successful missile launch. Ben is in paid work; he is economically active. His work has value and contributes, as part of the nuclear machine, to the nation's growth, wealth, and productivity. (Waring 1999, 13)

Waring's observation is applicable to this study of Embu women and broaches the deliberate patriarchal attitudes regarding the positive contribution of women to production. It also highlights the unrecognized and unappreciated contributions of Embu women in food production and depicts the exploitation of indigenous women by their male counterparts. In the following section I explore the everyday experiences of rural women and their gendered roles.

Within the Embu community, gender is an essential factor in crop cultivation. According to Mbilinyi (1997), gender relations are understood to be social constructs, not biological differences. They have a history, based on women's resistances and victories as well as subjugations and defeats. Mbilinyi (1997) asserts that gender analysis enables us to examine commonalities and differences among women, but also among men and between men and women, in order to understand gender oppression and to strategize for action. Mbilinyi (1997) points out that this approach has a transformative impact that stretches beyond the improvement of conditions for women and disempowered people; she describes how empowerment can result from liberating ourselves, through our own actions, on our own behalf. Gender therefore becomes an organizing factor in relation to the various foods that are grown by most Embu rural families.

Men normally cultivate cash crops such as sugar cane, yams, and bananas and keep beehives for honey. Women cultivate vegetables, grains, and legumes, which are consumed by the household. Thus, we see that where crops are commercially viable, men are the cultivators. Over the years, indigenous African women have placed family above personal interest. They have grown food to feed the family and, despite their busy daily activities, have helped their husbands to tend their crops, knowing that the proceeds from their sale will be for his own use. According to Kanini, a participant in my study, "there were specific crops that were traditionally identified with men. However, these have changed over the years and especially when any food grown is earmarked for sale. I used to grow just a few tomatoes and carrots for the family, but as soon as I increased the yield and started to sell them, my husband told me I should turn all the proceeds over to him. At first I objected, but then it became a source of problems. Now that I give him all the money, the fights have stopped."

The economic dominance of men is readily apparent. When any produce assumes commercial importance, it becomes a "male crop," but a crop grown for use in the home is a "female crop." Kanini also noted, "Do you see that plot with maize? That is my husband's. I use the plot behind this one to plant all the foods for my family. I plant maize, beans, and other vegetables all together. My husband does not intercrop."

The cultivation of fruit – oranges, mangoes, papayas, avocados, passion fruits, pears, lemons, and strawberries – is the purview of all members of the family, but if the fruit are grown in larger quantities for sale, their management is assumed by men, from planting to harvesting to selling. Men claim title to the fruit, which are generically referred to as *matunda*. Men decide how much should be sold or preserved, but rely on the women's ingenuity and knowledge for proper indigenous food preservation. If, however, a man decides to sell the entire harvest, it is the woman who ensures that the crop is prepared and delivered to the marketplace. Following the sale, he may buy a kilogram of meat for one-time cooking as a sign of appreciation for the work done by his wife or purchase a loaf of bread for the children.

The evidence of patriarchy is clear and evident in domestic relations. Male domination is part of the daily experience of women in the home and, by extension, within the community. Yet the women continue selflessly to meet their families' needs, often being compelled to abandon indigenous methods of planting and farming. They do not appreciate mono-cropping or planting in a straight line, because their intent is to utilize unused space in order to plant crops for domestic consumption. According to Wawira, "my concern is that I have the food planted on time and that I harvest enough food to feed my family. I usually intercrop to make sure that every space is used." Similarly, Marigu problematizes her husband's mono-cropping practices because they ignore usable space: "I find my husband wastes a lot of space by not agreeing to intercrop." Intercropping is preferable to mono-cropping because it also reduces the problem of weeds and ensures the raising of crops that have different maturing seasons. When the crops have matured and are ready for harvest, it becomes a time of labour intensity, requiring proper organization and planning. According to Ciarunji, "When you harvest your food, make sure it is completely dry; this way the moisture content is low. If you store your food when it is not completely dry, your food will grow mould and rot ... You can tell the moisture content by biting one grain, or feel it on your hand. It all comes with experience ... If you leave your food in the *shamba* and it gets rained on, you might lose it because it will absorb the water and start germinating."

As noted earlier, indigenous knowledges emanate from everyday experiences. It is this heuristic framework of learning through experiences that enables indigenous people to theorize their knowledge. This process enabled Ciarunji to draw conclusions from observation. To assume that indigenous knowledges lack predictability and a scientific basis is to downplay their effectiveness and authenticity. We see the wisdom of these women in Wawira's statement regarding the timing involved in food management: "If I am early or late in harvesting, threshing, or putting the preservatives, I could lose a lot of my food through spoilage and weevils ... I try to be on time, but sometimes you cannot help the situation." Often, events occur that require women to step outside their regular activities. Sometimes these circumstances prevent them from performing the harvesting and post-harvesting activities on time. Wawira confirms this: "If there is sickness in the family, a lot of other things suffer because all my attention is focused on the sick person. Or if my husband has had a good harvest, I spend a lot of time helping him to harvest and preserve the crop. Another thing that can hold me back is when I have just given birth ... it takes me about a month to recover completely and to resume my routine duties."

Indeed, indigenous African women cannot be constructed as the weaker vessel or as lazy. They work from dawn till dusk to make things comfortable for their families. They adjust to circumstances. It is this inherent nature and willingness to sacrifice that causes a typical Embu woman to suspend her own work to attend the sick or help her husband in his harvesting. As we see from Wawira, she will work up to the last day before she gives birth, and after delivery will take a short break and then resume her normal routine.

A significant portion of the women's time is allocated to the activities of planting, weeding, harvesting, and post-harvesting, which often impinge on other family chores. During these periods the family's food intake decreases. Some women have little time to prepare main meals; others, who do prepare them, will serve their families but, owing to fatigue, will not eat and will go to bed hungry. Another participant, Kanyiva comments: "Sometimes when I come from the *shamba*, I am too tired to cook ... If there are ripe bananas, I give them to my family and we sleep ... Sometimes I am too tired to eat even if I manage to cook for the family." This reality recounted by Kanyiva is not exclusive to Embu women. Kabeer (1991) indicates that in Zambia the family's eating habits are affected during the busy seasons of planting and harvesting when the women have to reorganize their daily routines. Wawira says: "I leave the house very early in the morning and I do not return home until evening. This can go on for two to three weeks until all the food has been harvested and brought home."

The daily schedule is normalized once all the food is safely stored. "Shelling maize or winnowing beans or millet can be done in the evening while cooking supper or socializing," says Wawira. From these women's narratives it is evident that daily schedules are not static; they change according to the season and need adjustment to conform to current situations.

The women with whom I talked were skilled in the management of harvested crops, knowing what food required dry conditions and how to air the storage space to prevent the crops from rotting. Different women had their own unique ways of drying the crops. Alice "spread the harvested food inside the granary for about a month for drying," while Wawira "spread the maize outside for a week to dry." Njura, however, waited until the maize was completely dry before harvesting it.

The majority of the women received little or no help from their husbands. Sometimes, if the harvest was good, they would ask female neighbours and their children to help. According to Kanini: "I usually do all this work alone, but during the holidays my children help me, and once in a while my husband assists me and especially if we are harvesting his crop. Occasionally I invite my friends to come and help ... I do not pay them any money, but I feed them and in return I help them. We have sayings: 'Scratch my back and I will scratch yours,' or 'Two hands are better than one.' If my friends or neighbours are not available, I hire casual labour for about a week. This is very rare because there hasn't been that much food, and labour is expensive." Hired labour is rare as most of these women live below the poverty line, and some derive their living from casual labour, in addition to doing their household chores. Although female neighbours and friends help with harvesting, threshing beans, and carrying maize to the homestead, they cannot help with shelling maize or applying preservatives. As Kaniva explained, "Friends or neighbours do not help you to thresh, winnow, or preserve your food. You do this at your own pace."

Through experience, Embu women know how long to keep their crops before they begin threshing, winnowing, or preserving, and they also know what should be attended to first and what can wait. Warue stated: "As soon as the beans are dry and ready for harvest, I have to uproot them and thresh them. Usually I winnow and put preservatives for each day's threshing. It is very rare that I store the beans with husks because this would mean double work. The work of maize is different. After the harvest I leave the maize cob in the granary for a couple of weeks so that it can dry." Threshing beans requires special preparation. For instance, when the beans are ready for harvesting, women select a special place in the *shamba*, and there, a week in advance of the threshing, they create a smooth, even surface, sometimes using a sisal mat or a canvas sheet. The threshing grounds for beans, peas, and millet are specially prepared, and when I asked Wachiuma to explain how this was done, she replied: "We did, and still do, all the threshing on well-smeared ground (*itiri*). This ground is prepared in the middle of the *shamba* by smearing it with cow dung mixed with ashes ... If the floor chips a little bit, you have to make some cow-dung paste and mend the broken floor, and otherwise your millet or beans would get dirty."

The younger women did not know how to prepare the threshing ground and had to depend on their mothers or mothers-in-law to prepare the grounds for them. Others had to save money to make sure they had the threshing sheet. The threshing ground costs nothing but time. According to Njura, "These grounds are things of the past, and we have to try to adapt to the changes. Money is a big problem, but then you can work for other people as casual labour for a week and get some cash." The young women save their meagre resources and buy a threshing sheet in order to keep up with the times.

Women spend between three and eight hours a day carrying out these post-harvest activities. When enough or all of the beans have been uprooted, the threshing begins with the women using long wooden sticks, or *mivoro*, prepared by men. According to Wachiuma, "The man of the house knows the sizes to prepare for his woman – not too heavy and not too light." Wachiuma continued her explanation: "The stalk hitting would go on until all the beans have been removed from the kernel ... you would know when this happens because of the noise made by the stalk. If you are not very experienced with this process, you could end up throwing away your food." When all the threshing for the day has been completed, the winnowing starts. Wachiuma describes the process: "To carry out the winnowing process you have to check the direction of the wind and stand with your back to the wind. When all the winnowing is done, then you decide the amounts to be stored, consumed, and given out to neighbours ... giving to neighbours depends on what type of neighbours you have."

By holding a maize cob in their hands and biting the grain, they can tell whether the moisture content is high or low. By standing on the threshold, they can tell whether the day is good for winnowing, threshing, or drying food produce.[1] These findings are similar to Weikiya's (1992) research findings on shea butter extraction among women in Ghana. The Ghanaian women use their hands to determine the quality and quantity of the final product. Post-harvest activities require planning; daily routines have to be reorganized, and the threshing grounds have to be readied ahead of time. Timing is crucial. The women recognize and are familiar with the steps to be taken. Most emphasize the concept of timing for they know that if the harvesting is done too early or too late, the result could be rotten food. Proper handling of the produce is important throughout all stages, from harvesting to preservation to storage. Sometimes, however, factors such as sickness, early rain, a husband's crop, or childbirth may interfere.

When all goes well, when every stage goes like the proverbial clockwork, food preparation then becomes the next step, as Wawira noted in her interview in 1993-4: "I feed my family with the food in season, but mostly it is maize and beans. Sometimes I cook mashed bananas and potatoes, some other vegetable food, and at other times *muthugo* ... if I have maize flour, I prepare *ugali* and porridge. Mmm! At Christmas I may prepare rice and meat."

Among the Embu community the main foods are a mixture of maize and beans (*githeri*); green bananas and potatoes (*gitoero*); a vegetable dish (*nyenyi*); cassava and potatoes boiled together (*runyugu*); split maize mixed with beans or peas (*muthugo*); stiff porridge (*ugali*); and various vegetables including arrowroot, yam, and cassava. These last three items are no longer easily available as people have stopped planting them. Meat, rice, and chapatti, which are not indigenous to the Embu (they were introduced by the Indians who used to own shops in most Embu villages), are rare delicacies usually eaten during celebrations. The home-made traditional porridge (*uchuru*) has also become rare because of the changes in lifestyle and the demands on women's time. Cucu cannot see the logic of abandoning indigenous foods and spending money on items such as tea leaves, coffee, maize flour, and salt, traditionally prepared by women. According to Cucu, nature has provided for the needs of humans, but sadly this is ignored in the name of change and advancement. It is important to note that local vegetables contain the necessary nutritional value required by the body. For example, *Biden pilosa* (*mucege*) has calcium; *Oxygonum sinuatum* (*nthaugu*) has vitamin A; *Commelina benghalensis* (*mukengeria*) has iron; *Amaranthus dubius* (*terere*) has 8 per cent protein and 4 per cent carbohydrates, as well as calcium, iron, and vitamins B and C; cowpea (*Vigna unguiculata*) (*mathoroko*) is in the family of beans that is very high in protein; pumpkin (*Cucurbita maxima*) (*marenge*) contains 1 per cent protein and 8 per cent carbohydrates, and the dried seeds contain 23 per cent protein, 21 per cent carbohydrates, and up to 50 per cent oil. (For more information see Maundu et al. 1999 and International Plant Genetic Resources Institute [IPGRI] 1997). These vegetables are disease and draught resistant. However, they have been replaced by exotic foods such as cabbage, kale, and carrots, which are not indigenous to the Embu. It is interesting to note that the older women felt that the younger generation could not prepare some of the indigenous foods such as porridge because, as Cucu said, "your age-mates cannot use a grinding stone. They cannot hold a pestle properly. What do [they learn] ... in schools? I do not know what happens when you leave us and go to school. Your hands lose the grip to hold." Traditionally brewed beer (*njovi ya muratina*), made from honey, sugar cane, or sugar, is common at local bars. Although it is illegal to make local brews at home, some women risk arrest and make the beer to supplement their meagre incomes. The brewing of beer is only allowed in homes during ceremonies such as weddings, the birth of a child, circumcision, and fund-raising. For such occasions the chief of the area has to give a written permit.

Women learn to prepare traditional foods from an early age, and therefore most women were amazed when I asked them to explain to me how these foods were prepared. For them it was "common-sense" knowledge. As Mama puts it, "learning to prepare and cook our foods starts the minute you are born. You observe from your mother's back. You hear your mother giving instructions to your older sisters on how to cook. You accompany her everywhere, from birth until you get married or go to school. By the time you are ten years you can prepare it without any assistance, and you say you want me to tell you how to prepare it? I did not know that there are women who cannot cook *githeri*." When women (I among them) migrate to the cities, they tend to lose a sense and practice of the rural ways of living. In Western society the cooking arts are mostly acquired through professional schools, the duplication of recipes from cookbooks, or through the print and electronic media. To Embu women, these avenues of learning are quite surprising because learning to cook is integral to childhood experiences, and women are expected to have acquired this knowledge as a normal part of growing up. It would be embarrassing to any woman and her parents if she matured into puberty and eventual adulthood without this basic skill.

Almost all the Embu women with whom I spoke during my research found observation and imitation during socializing to be a natural process. Boys are excluded from this process in which girls are being educated to eschew idleness and learn how to feed their families. In fact, it is offensive for boys to be found loitering around the kitchen during food preparation. One may wonder whether this male exclusion from domestic chores makes Embu women unwitting participants in the reproduction of patriarchal mindsets in future generations.

Towards Indigenous Reconception of Time

In the wisdom of indigenous Embu women, time is not a doctrine that binds. It can be said that they use time and do not waste time because it is measured by the accomplishment of tasks. The sense of time is captured in the *Song of Lawino*, which, even though it deals with Ugandan realities, applies to Embu women's relationship with time: "I do not know / how to keep the white man's time / My mother taught me / the way of the Acoli." The world of the indigenous Embu woman does not revolve around a Western concept of time. Okot p'Btiek words are echoed in Mbithi's (2012) keynote speech in which he indicates that time is tied to the belief and behaviour system of African people. Mbithi explains that when you talk of now (*sasa*), it binds people together, and in most time there is no reference of the future. When the woman in *Song of Lawino* is told that she does not know how to keep time by using the clock, she is justified because, within the African concept, time is measured according to events and experience. That is what I experienced when I talked to the Embu women during my research. Things are done when necessary, and not necessarily to meet a deadline. Among the Embu, if a task is not completed in a day, it is continued the following day. Social relations and communal interaction are not sacrificed in the name of meeting a deadline. The nature of social relations requires that a friend, a relative, or a distant relative – or even a stranger – can knock at one's door any time of the day, and customs and traditions demand that all work stop and the reason for the visit be ascertained before continuing. Nevertheless, many Embu women are multitaskers by nature. According to Kanyiva, a woman cannot afford to wait until she is completely "free" before she can start something new: "You cannot wait until you are completely free to prepare and cook *githeri*. You see, I took this opportunity as we talk to prepare the ingredients for tomorrow's *githeri*. That way, I do not feel I am not doing something useful. As a woman you cannot sit with your hands folded and talk ... you learn to focus on many things at the same time and never have your hands idle. Do you remember when you came in, I had to remove the *githeri* from the fire to make a cup of tea for you? You have to plan for interruptions, and that is why I place *githeri* on the fire as soon as the fire is free."

In fact, most of the respondents found it intriguing when I asked them how long it took them to complete a particular task. During my interview sessions with Cucu I found that she would be shelling maize, selecting beans, or peeling potatoes. I was keen to know how long it took her to have the maize or beans ready to be placed on the fire. She looked at me and said, "I do not wear a watch, and even if I do, I will not know how to tell time. I use the sun or shadows of trees to know what time it is." It is amazing to witness how these women synchronize their lives with nature. It was by putting this information on paper that I arrived at the average number of hours that the Embu women took to prepare the ingredients and the food. For most, it was an average of four hours including the cooking of the main meals. Regarding time taken for food preparation, Kanyiva said: "I can only estimate. Preparation of ingredients may take an hour or less, and actual cooking may take three to four hours. This preparation goes hand in hand with other household chores. For instance, while cleaning the beans or maize, I could be cooking tea, porridge, or visiting with a friend ... and when I place the *githeri* on the fire, I can leave it cooking and go to the farm or go to fetch water or collect firewood or collect fodder for the cows. Cooking *githeri* does not tie you down, and especially if you have children whom you can instruct while keeping an eye on the pot on the fire. When you do not have children, then you have to do it yourself." We thus see preparation and cooking as normal routines carried out concurrently with other household activities. These women do not have a stove with several burners, and this is perfectly suitable because it allows the women to easily estimate how long it will take for the food to be ready. Also, leaving the food cooking while they go about other tasks is not a problem; the energy released through the use of firewood is gradually reduced, and the food is left cooking through the warmth of the burning charcoal. When I asked Mama to explain her cooking experience, she responded: "Through experience you learn how long you will be gone before you come back to check on the food that is cooking. You measure the amount of water, the quality of the firewood, and estimate how long you will need to be away. All this comes with practice."

These women's narratives show that household chores carried out at a comfortable pace are not so tightly scheduled that they cannot be interrupted. Children are assigned duties at an early age, which teaches them responsibility. We see that the women emphasize experience. They know how long it takes for water to dry out of a cooking pot; they know how long the fire will burn before it requires rekindling. These knowledges, along with myriad others, become internalized.

Although cooking is an important component of women's daily activities, it is interwoven with other household chores. With some women, the ingredients needed for the following day's meals are prepared the night before, as Kanyiva explains: "I usually get all the ingredients for *githeri* the previous night unless I am too tired, then I soak the mixture before going to bed. When I prepare these ingredients in the morning, I do it between preparation of breakfast, feeding my husband and children, milking, and cleaning or visiting with friends. This makes my morning very hectic." Embu women have to be very conscious of how to manage time efficiently. Although they are seldom given credit for doing so, their time-management skills are superb. Njura summarized the issue of work and time: "It is hard to talk of time and work around the house. I believe the important thing is not how long it takes to complete a certain job or how long *githeri* will take to get ready; it is how well the job gets done and that everything you are required to do gets done. This is an art you acquire through experience and also through many years of observation when growing up." It becomes clear that, although time is a precious commodity, Embu women know how to make good use of it, and it does not cause them stress. Cooking, as we have seen, consumes a lot of the women's energies. However, those who have young children may delegate some aspects of the cooking to them while the rest of the family goes to the *shamba*. The children make certain that the fire does not go out and the food does not burn. If we extrapolate these women's organizational skills from the household to the corporate world – if the site is viewed as a new corporate body – we can see that their knack for efficient multitasking is something to be envied.

Food preservation, when necessary, is also a component of their skill set. Most of the women who were interviewed made enough food for one or two meals and did not have elaborate ways of preserving cooked foods. However, since *githeri* is frequently eaten, they have to know how to preserve it for a week. Things have changed for these women, and it has become difficult, if not impossible, to preserve their foods for a longer period. Ciarunji recalled with nostalgia: "When I was growing up, all foods could be preserved for a week or more. But not these days. Then, all the food would be scooped from the earthen pot and placed on the winnower [which separates the chaff from the grain]. The winnower would be kept in a dry place within the reach of all the children." Since most homesteads today do not have refrigeration facilities, the women must prepare their meals daily. Any leftovers are served on the following day to avoid spoilage and wastage. Unfortunately, despite the time that the women spend in tending and harvesting crops, preparing and preserving food, and taking care of all the household duties, the men place little value on women's work and efforts and expect the work to be done.

Another facet that cannot be ignored, and one that assumes crucial importance, is the social aspect of food as power. Food is central to many family occasions and is important to the social milieu in both nuclear and extended families. Food items can be viewed as symbolizing important social relations of power and subordination that exist within the family. These items function towards maintaining and reproducing a specific aspect of social order in the family and are typified by age and gender divisions that characterize them. The ways in which power is distributed along the lines of age and gender are beyond the scope of this research as they are very complex and warrant their own thorough examination.

One of the important family functions of indigenous Embu women is to provide proper food for consumption (Charles and Kerr 1988). This role is fundamental to the identity of indigenous Embu women and is a vital link to other family members. The implication is that Embu women exercise a certain level of power over the family, and this power is reflected in the day-to-day decisions about processing food for consumption or preservation. However, the power is not absolute. Embu women do not even have absolute control over the family's food supply. Food-processing practices help to maintain and reinforce a coherent ideology of the family throughout the social structure. During harvests the women's and the men's skills are complementary; men make indigenous technology and women put it to practical use. Women's organizational and managerial skills are quite evident as they take charge of the food processing.

The women without men in their homestead ask the men in their neighbourhood to make tools for them. Usually such services are paid with a bowl of porridge. Women are allowed to test the tool, and, if necessary, a modification is made. During the harvest, women's knowledge of food processing is highly valued. It is the women who know when all the grains have been threshed from their stalks, which family members are competent enough to take part in food-processing activities, when there is enough wind to remove the chaff through winnowing, when the threshing ground is ready, and when it needs repair. Once the grains have been cleaned, it is the women who decide the mode of storage.

Women's knowledge of the land and weather conditions gives them a superior position in food processing. Without relying on radio forecasts, they ascertain whether the day will be appropriate for harvesting, threshing, or winnowing the grains. By standing on the threshold of their homestead and taking in the totality of their environment, the women determine the day's suitability. Indigenous Kenyan women, therefore, play a central role in food production, processing, and storage.

Yet these women are neither included nor consulted when food policies are planned and implemented. This is mainly due to gender discrimination and the notion that women do not know; in addition, they are not part of the decision making on major issues that concern their communities such as government food policies. When government officials address farmers' meetings, they never direct their queries, concerns, or advice to women farmers – a situation that helps to explain Kenya's intermittent food shortages. This is not to say that such shortages have been due only to the absence of women's expertise but that the loss of women's expertise has had significant negative repercussions.

Owing to food shortages the Kenyan government has been monitoring food production and consumption patterns. It has created a national food policy (see *Sessional Paper no. 4* of 1981) that aims to establish self-sufficiency in food production by providing incentives such as higher prices for produce. Nevertheless, the country has faced sporadic shortages of the main foods – maize, wheat, rice, and milk. The situation has arisen even though the production levels of these foods in most cases exceed 1960s levels, when surpluses were common. The shortages may be attributed to the population's high growth rate. In order to be self-sufficient in food production, Kenya needs to maintain a 4.9 per cent growth in food production. This means that the rate of food production should be approximately 1 per cent higher than the rate of population growth. If this expanding food-production rate is not achieved, the government will have to continue importing basic foods. The most severe food shortage was experienced in 2011.

Food sufficiency is inextricably linked to agricultural development, improved processing technology, and preservation. The government's plans during the past forty-five years have placed great emphasis on food production by small-scale farmers and the mobilization of domestic resources for equitable development. Unfortunately, those plans have failed to mobilize domestic resources, use local knowledge and strategies, or alleviate poverty among the rural poor. Whenever there is a good harvest, small-scale farmers continue to lose their food crops because of poor storage facilities, lack of transport, and fear, on the part of many farmers, of using indigenous technology for food preservation.

Research reveals that although the government has neglected the knowledge base of rural populations, rural men and women often still use their indigenous preservation practices when they need money. There has to be a governmental reconnection with this local base if food shortages, such as those experienced during the last forty-five years, are to be overcome. The contribution of women is not only vital for household maintenance but also essential for a successful national policy on food.

With an increasing population and diminishing agricultural land, it has become clear that there is an imbalance between food supply and demand, consequently requiring systematic food management to control or eliminate shortages. The government has encouraged people to store surplus grain and has instituted a price-control policy to stabilize the production and price of food in Kenya. Currently, approximately 62 per cent of the total maize production in Kenya is retained on the farms for subsistence and is stored in cribs and bins. However, research indicates that storage losses to the farms from these systems are as high as 26 per cent. Although the government has encouraged farmers to use tested storage facilities, only a few farmers have done so; most lack the money to purchase these facilities. It was also noted in my study that some women, especially those in their twenties, did not know indigenous forms of food preservation. Others feared that their neighbours would think of them as poor if they were discovered using indigenous methods to preserve farm produce.

The research further noted that firewood collection and water fetching are important practices among Embu women. In most cases, the ability to fetch water quickly or collect firewood when necessary largely affects the time spent on food preparation and other domestic chores. Some women fetch water in the morning and collect firewood in the evening; others make these two chores their last jobs before returning home to prepare the evening meal. The collection of water and firewood is interwoven with other domestic or farming activities. Ciarunji, the elderly woman introduced earlier, collected her water very early in the morning: "If we have no water, I wake up before everybody else to go to the river to fetch water. When you do that, you collect clean water. If you wait until everybody starts going to the river, you collect dirty water. People from upstream make the water dirty for us ... they wash their clothes, bathe ... I like getting my water before it gets spoiled."

Embu women can determine the cleanliness of water by looking at its colour. They are also aware of some of the water-borne diseases and may want to boil the water before using it, especially if they have reason to believe that the water is not clean. However, since time is of the essence to these women, and they may not have enough time or even firewood to boil unclean water, many prefer to fetch water very early in the morning or late in the evening to reduce the possibilities of fetching unclean water. Water filters are unheard of, and, even if they were available, many families would not be able to afford them. The fact that these women have not heard of water filters does not mean that they do not employ indigenous ways of purifying water. Ciarunji used an indigenous earthen pot to store water and filter out impurities. According to her, "the pot keeps the water cool, and the clay absorbs all the dirt from the water. I learned this from my mother."

Women fetch water whenever the need arises. If the water in the house runs out during the night, water fetching is given top priority the following day. If the water is not enough for the day, women collect more on their way home from the farm. The rate of water consumption depends on what is being cooked and the chores at hand. In case there are visitors, or clothes need to be washed, the women have to make extra trips to the river. The distance covered by Embu women to fetch water ranges from one to six kilometres, which takes usually between an hour and five hours depending on one's proximity to the water source and the time of year. Ninety per cent of the respondents got their water from either a river or a well, while 4 per cent got their water from rain-catchment points but had to supplement their supply. Rain-catchment water is mostly available during the rainy season, but much of this water is wasted because most women do not have large, reliable storage facilities. Piped water was supplied on a communal basis, but not every house had this facility. Although the pipe-borne water appeared to be clear, there were still doubts about its cleanliness. According to the women, the pipe-borne water had a funny taste and could not quench their thirst. In addition, the water is turned off from time to time, thus making the pipes an unreliable source of water. Potable water is government controlled and is often turned off each day to "build up" pressure; the frequency with which it is turned off is largely determined by the season. For instance, during the dry season the pipe-borne water is frequently turned off. Besides the unreliability of the pipe-borne water, the women have to consider the time spent to acquire it. It is not unusual to see long queues of women trying to fetch water. Since time is very important to these women, they usually do not entertain the thought of waiting for water.

Firewood collection was another demanding activity, and this too varied from season to season. During maize shelling most families use maize cobs as a source of energy, supplementing the firewood needed for homes. Since the maize is shelled during the dry season, women usually spend fewer hours in search of firewood at that time. However, the story is completely different during the rainy season, when it takes women twice the amount of time that they would take during the dry season to search for firewood. The study revealed that all the respondents used firewood for cooking and for warming the house. However, the use of charcoal is rare. Only 5 per cent of women in the Embu community use charcoal to supplement firewood.[2]

As already noted, the collection of firewood and water is interwoven with other household chores. Women can sometimes leave food to cook while they search for firewood or fetch water. These activities consume women's time, energy, and resources. During the dry season the social organization of women's daily routines changes to suit the conditions and the tasks at hand. Often, some rivers dry up, making the fetching of water more time consuming.

A closer examination of household chores indicates that during the planting season women reduce the time allotted to cooking. Women also spend less time searching for firewood during this season because crop planting is tiresome and time consuming. At other times, when water and firewood are scarce, women cook foods that do not consume too much water.

The type of housing available to each family determines the time spent by each household on cleaning and repairing and on collecting water. According to one respondent, part of the maintenance exercise is to smear a mixture of cow dung and ashes every other week on the house. This particular exercise is time consuming and requires extra gallons of water. Momsen (1991) also found that thatched roofs, earthen walls, and floors require constant repair. Kabeer (1991) reported that studies carried out in Zimbabwe show that the nutritional level is low during the height of harvesting or planting, when women have to travel long distances in search of water or firewood, or when food is scarce.

From the foregoing it is evident that Embu women are overburdened. From harvesting cash crops to growing food for household use, they work very hard each day. This is how Kanini summarizes her daily routine:

> I wake up before sunrise and pray. After which I sweep the kitchen and the compound, make fire, prepare breakfast, milk the cows, prepare my husband's water for wiping his face, prepare the ingredients for midday meal, leave the food cooking, and go to the farm. At 12:00 p.m. I go back home to get the midday meal ready for the children. At 1:00 p.m. I go back to the *shamba* until 4:00 p.m.; then I go to look for firewood and to fetch water. I get back home just before the sun sets to prepare the evening meal. After my husband and children have eaten and slept, I take my supper, clean up, and try to be in bed by 10:00 p.m.[3]

For Alice, her responsibility at home includes milking the cattle and delivering milk to the Kenya Creameries Company (KCC). "The church bell wakes me up. As soon as it rings, I wake up, boil the water for milking. After that I take the milk to the dairy ... which is about four kilometres away. I have to be there before 6:30 a.m. so that the milk can be weighed and recorded. After 6:30 a.m. they turn us back ... that is a big loss, and my husband will not be happy with me."

These women portrayed dedication and selflessness. They denied themselves rest, sleep, and food for the sake of their families. Sometimes I think about their dedication, especially to their husbands, and wonder whether it is out of fear, respect, or tradition, or all of the above. According to Kanini, "I feed my husband, then the children, and I eat after everyone else." For most women there was no specific reason that husbands and children were fed first except that it was a tradition. As Kanini noted, "This is a tradition; my mother did it, and I do not see why I should not do it. I guess it shows you respect him and care for your children. I try to follow what I used to see my mother doing."

The hours that these women spent on work and the tedious nature of their tasks had serious health implications. Most of the women complained of backaches, chronic coughs, and pains in their joints. There is no doubt that the heavy loads they carry on their back each day, while their babies are strapped to their front, have contributed to the chronic backaches. The chronic coughs could be attributed to daily exposure to the cold morning air that they have to brave on their way to collect water or fodder. In most instances these women would be thinly dressed, and in spite of the fact that Kenya is in the tropics, the temperatures in the Embu area can drop to zero during the period from June to August. The hands and feet of these women bore testimony to their daily struggles. Their feet were rough and heavily etched with deep grooves as a result of walking barefoot thousands of kilometres each year to accomplish their daily chores.

In spite of all their efforts, indigenous women's contributions have been undervalued and discounted. The government of Kenya needs to consult both men and women when it comes to food policies and not just depend on what the men report at village meetings. Imam (1997, 26) notes the importance of using proper analytical tools that speak to the realities of African women. This is particularly essential when addressing issues of power between genders. According to Imam, the need is not only to understand power dynamics between genders but also to produce a "form of knowledge that can help transform oppressive realities" in Africa. Most participants in this study indicated that their spouse saw them as property. Embu women's daily itinerary is filled with tasks that contribute to the comfort of their husbands and families, yet these tasks are undervalued and unappreciated because what the women value, the men count as nothing. For instance, every day the female members of the family will wake up early to fetch water, prepare breakfast, and feed the cows or goats. These chores are performed not only by the mature women in the family but also by the young girls (Wane and Gathenya 2003). There have been numerous writings on gender imbalance when it comes to the household chores in some Kenyan homes. Recognition and appreciation of what these women know and do will enhance their self-respect, their self-confidence, and their sense of power, pride, and success.

4 Food Preservation and Change

Boxall (1989) shows that in countries where farming is predominantly at the subsistence level, an estimated 60–70 per cent of the cereal and grain produced is retained at the farm. Farmers must conserve enough grain to feed both family and livestock from one harvest to the next. Storage methods have evolved according to local customs and social and economic conditions and have become associated with certain varieties of grain. Newcomers to a community who are unfamiliar with post-harvest activities may erroneously conclude that these methods are inefficient and wasteful compared to mechanized processes.

Farmers ensure that the grain is not infested with insects and not threshed before it is completely dry. This requires organization along with knowledge of the grain and its suitable harvesting time. Premature harvesting results in rotting caused by high-moisture content, or the food may acquire toxins that are harmful to the body. A late harvest can lead to grain that is spoiled by animals, microorganisms, and insects. Changes in moisture content that are precipitated by rapid or over-drying can also lead to the grain cracking and create conditions for infestation. Proper drying is important for storage. For example, in southern Ghana, a raised platform on which unsheathed maize cobs are placed is used to dry the grain. In East Africa, "cribs" made of wood or bamboo are used both as storage and drying places (Boxall 1989).

Sometimes, even when all the above conditions are observed, grains will rot and become infested. An efficiently managed storage facility is essential; it should protect grain from rain and ground moisture, have controlled humidity and temperature, and be resistant to insects and rodents.

A variety of indigenous storage systems have evolved in developing countries to satisfy local requirements. Although basic concepts may seem similar, construction methods and appearance vary according to particular conditions and customs. In most cases storage facilities are constructed with plant materials, mud, or stone. Facilities are often on above-ground platforms. If the harvested crop does not require a large storage facility, containers such as baskets, clay pots, gourds, or drums are used. In some instances sacks are also used. The type of facility is determined by local crop patterns. In areas where two or more crops can be grown annually, the farm needs only a temporary storage facility, one capable of holding sufficient grain to last until the next harvest. In other areas where rains are unpredictable and there is only one yearly harvest, more permanent storage is required.

The introduction of new grains and legumes has also expanded indigenous techniques for food conservation. Some newer grains grow faster than do the indigenous grains, disturb the food cycle, and disrupt certain seasonal activities. New grains can also be less resistant to insect attack and more vulnerable to spoilage. Farmers who have tried a new hybrid variety of grains often experience problems with indigenous conservation methods. Their only alternative has been insecticides, the cost of which is beyond the reach of the majority of farmers, especially women. In light of these factors, Boxall (1989) concludes that efforts to introduce better storage facilities for new breeds have met resistance from local populations in some places in Africa.

Embu rural women use a range of preservation methods from drying to the use of pesticides, ashes, marigolds, hot peppers, onions, cow dung, garlic, trash, and aromatic leaves. The type of method selected depends on the food being preserved, and the success of the procedure depends on who manages the crop from harvesting to storage. As Ciarunji stated, "What I use depends on the food being preserved. For instance, I use marigold for maize, and for beans and potatoes I use ashes." Mama said, "I use whatever is available. Sometimes ashes, other times paraffin or soil." Angelina said, "Most of the time I use pesticide. It is only when there is no money that I use these natural preservatives."

According to these women there is no specific preservative that is used in food preservation. The range is wide. Only 14 per cent of the women I interviewed used pesticides, while 75 per cent relied on natural preservatives. The research data shows the following distribution: 15 per cent used marigolds and other indigenous repellents; 5 per cent used hot peppers; 29 per cent used ashes; 6 per cent used cow dung; only 1 per cent used soil as a preservative. The remainder used a mixture of the above methods.

It becomes more interesting when one looks at the age distribution of the participants and their response to using natural or artificial preservatives. While almost 95 per cent of those aged twenty to twenty-nine preferred artificial (pesticides) to natural preservatives, the group aged fifty and above preferred natural methods. Some of the younger women who used pesticides thought that it was backward and outdated to preserve food using indigenous practices. According to Wangeci: "What would my neighbours say if they found out that I use marigold or ashes to preserve food? They would laugh at me and think I am old fashioned." Njura also noted: "Indigenous practices are time consuming and tedious ... However, the good thing about these preservatives is that they are free. ... and they are also chemical free, and during the time of scarcity, people turn to these herbs to preserve their food, but they do not talk about it, because they are embarrassed."

This finding raises valid questions about the future of indigenous knowledges, especially given the high impact of modernity on food preservation. As noted from the comments of Wangeci and Njura, younger-generation women think that it is backward and primitive to employ indigenous food-processing methods, and those who do use them make it clear that they do not want their neighbours to know, because they will be ridiculed. It seems that the younger generations are more concerned about losing face with their neighbours than with the harmful effects of pesticides. Ironically, and by contrast, the older women are comfortable with indigenous methods of food preservation and do not care how their interest in them is received by their neigbours. The older generation gravitates towards indigenous methods of food preservation owing to its simplicity and familiarity. According to Ciarunji, the natural processes are no different from the new changes, particularly if one plans ahead: "All you need to do is plan. For example, if you want to use ashes, start early to collect it, and whenever you are not busy, clean it, sieve it so that when your food is ready for preserving, you scoop ashes and mix it with your food ... just like you do with pesticide." Warue also argues that careful and timely planning can reduce the stress that comes with indigenous methods of food preservation: "You plan ahead of time and harvest your ashes and get them ready for your food ... You cannot leave it up to the last minute [or] you will not have time to prepare and use it. Marigolds used to grow everywhere, but this is not the case anymore because most of the land has been cultivated."

Warue's comment also raises a very critical question: Are the indigenous methods of food preservation sustainable, given the changes in environment and the younger generations' strong desire for modernity? The challenges facing the custodians of indigenous practices include not only dealing with the reluctance of the current generation to acquire their knowledges but also protecting them from extinction. Rwamba, a participant, argues that the clearing of bushes has robbed farmers of the local herbs and other repellants that used to be easily accessible in the past. Forests and pastures that provide diverse medicines, fruits, herbs for tea, edible leaves, and leaves that produce foam for washing clothes, along with firewood, are threatened by deforestation. Similarly, women who eke out a living for their families through cultivation and knowledgeable use of wild plants and animals now have to increase the time spent searching for these resources during the dry season. This change in the use of time requires new thinking and a response in order to keep alive the knowledge about indigenous food preservation.

Could it be that these older women are still attached to indigenous methods of food preservation because they are not amiable to changes? Perhaps that is a factor; however, a critical look at their position suggests that there is also an element of resistance to wholesale acceptance of foreign influence that may have negative repercussions. For instance, Cucu, besides her preference for indigenous methods, sees no sense in using foreign powders to preserve food: "I cannot stand the pesticide scent nor eat any foods preserved with it." Cucu does not understand why the younger generation "rushes" into things without first testing them. She could recall the days when food was stored without preservatives: "There were no weevils or worms to destroy food. The only thing that women used to worry about was rotting ... but if your food was completely dry, then it could stay for two seasons." Warue insisted that she and her age group have not used pesticide to preserve their food, because they do not see any need to abandon the traditional methods of food preservation: "I do not see why I should start using pesticides now. Besides, pesticides are not given out free." Another participant, Wanja, argued that she has refrained from using the pesticides because of the cost involved in acquiring them: "I would like to use pesticides but cannot afford them, and since my mother uses ashes, I have learnt the process from her." Although Wanja is using the traditional methods of food preservation, she has hidden this knowledge from her friends and neighbours for fear that she may become a laughing stock.

It appears that the high interest generated towards pesticides and other Western methods of food preservation by the younger generations has everything to do with class and prestige rather than effectiveness. For the younger generations, the ability to use pesticides denotes their economic status. Yet research in North America has shown the harmful effects of these chemical preservatives on humans and ecosystems (Shiva, 2000). Embu women have traditionally carried knowledge of the health benefits related to foodstuffs that are produced and stored using natural methods of food preservation (that is, organic food). Unfortunately, this knowledge is not always accessible to the younger generations of the Embu community. The result is an uncritical and mass adoption of Western, inorganic methods of food growth and preservation at the expense of the rich, local, organic means. How then can the younger generation of Embu women grow to understand and maintain the traditions of their elders? Certainly there is a pressing need to educate them away from their current trend of thought. There is also a need to improve the traditional methods of food preservation to make them more accommodating and attractive to the younger generation.

Beyond these issues, however, there is the reality that colonial education continues to pose a threat to indigenous knowledge and upbringing. It seems that the more the younger generations are exposed to Western education, the more they distance themselves from anything relating to indigenous knowledge. Jeremy Seabrook (1993) noted that the economic reform packages introduced by the IMF and the World Bank to Africa have positioned the West as the "bringer" of enlightenment, charity, and humanity which promises to share with local captives the secret of Western wealth creation. This fresh mutation makes all earlier colonial experiments seem crude and archaic. In some sense, the actual damage of these economic reforms is done by their ability to corrupt and undermine the indigenous identity of local learners such that the latter consider anything foreign to be the true basis of society. National pride is at a low ebb; the younger generations of Embu women seem to have a general distaste for indigenous knowledge and practices. How did these economic reforms succeed in making them consumers of Western products? It started with aid and grants. As with drugs, the process of becoming addicted is gradual, but once one is hooked, it becomes difficult to be untangled. All foreign goods that Europeans and the Western world continue to shower on Africans in the name of foreign aid are part of the process of building the future desire for such products.

The solution to the Embu's challenge lies in reconstructing the local identity of young Embu women. Until we deconstruct the insatiable desire for foreign goods, which is becoming part of the identity of the young Embu generation, the entire struggle to liberate ourselves will be in vain. The battle for economic reform must start in the mind. Until the identity of the young generation is built on Embu indigenous knowledge, even the world's money will not be able to recover our economy.

As Kenya inches its way forward, it is important that our national conversation be open to the possibility of deconstructing the structures that were initially established by colonial masters. This calls for openness, sincerity, and respect for views that may differ from the standard ideas acquired from the colonialists. Today we are living in a world where some of the colonial thoughts must undergo serious revision or be altogether abandoned. Either we devise ideas that will create a space for us in which we can manoeuvre to escape these unpleasant circumstances or we ascend new mountains and climb deep old valleys of colonial mindsets in order to see the fulfilment of the grand visions of our elders. According to the great philosopher and political economist John Stuart Mill, when society needs to be rebuilt, there is no use in attempting to rebuild it on the old plan. To move forward as a nation, it is important to deconstruct the old. We must continue to reform the education system in Kenya to make room for local knowledge, values, world views, and practices. Dei (2000a) conceptualizes *indigenous knowledge* as knowledge associated with long-term occupancy of a place. It refers to the traditional norms and social values as well as the mental constructs that guide, organize, and regulate a people's way of living and making sense of their world. It is the sum experience and knowledge of a given social group that forms the basis of decision making in the face of familiar and unfamiliar problems and challenges. Indigenous knowledge is always transmitted to the next generation to ensure the survival of that generation in its environment. When a generation concentrates its search for survival knowledge on "strangers" rather than on its elders, it ends up placing square pegs in round holes. Education should be transformative and sensitive to the natural environment. The indigenous knowledge recognizes the world in a holistic manner, and therefore it helps us to understand that our actions and inactions can cause damage to nature.

Understandingly, some of the indigenous knowledge needs to undergo revision for current consumption; however, there is a meaningful difference between critical interrogation of indigenous knowledge and wholesale rejection of indigenous knowledge. Until we open ourselves to the process of acquiring indigenous knowledge and incorporating it into formal schooling, we will be losing our national identity and walking in the shadows of the colonial masters.

According to Wachiuma, the art of preserving food takes more than experience in cooking. While it may be easier to perform the latter, the former involves considerable apprenticeship.

> Cooking is not difficult; however, to preserve food you had to learn from your mother or aunts through observation. We never had weevils. We started having problems with the weevils soon after the Second World War. After harvesting, we kept everything in *miruru* [a container woven from twigs and plastered with a mixture of cow dung and ashes] or hung the maize on branches. This food could stay there until the next season. Those days the seasons never changed ... we knew when it would rain so we did not fear that the food would be destroyed if it were left on the *shamba* to dry. These days you cannot do that. If it is not the weevils, the moths, or the worms, the rains will destroy your food or it will be stolen from your *shamba*.

For Wachiuma, insufficient or wrong methods of food preservation can lead to starvation for the entire family; however, if mistakes occur, they are easily corrected. It is suspected that weevils were either brought back by soldiers returning from the war in Europe or borne on the various crops introduced by the colonizers. The true origin of the weevils remains unclear.

At first, women did not know how to respond to the problem of weevils and moths. According to Ciarunji, it was through trial and error that Embu women were able to find antidotes to weevil and worm infestations: "Through trial and error we learnt that various leaves could be used as repellents for weevils and worms. Marigold, lantana camara (*mucimoro*), and other shrubs and bushes became very important once we got to know that they could be used to preserve food." The women did not stop exploring other possibilities, and, as Rwamba put it, "by the time the fight for independence was declared, most women knew that ashes, cow dung, and soil could be used as preservatives." Times have changed as well as the seasons. The natural environment has been destroyed. The older women learned from their mothers, and they knew they could rely on their acquired skills. These women have the capacity to solve many of their environmental needs, but their children question their capabilities. The government has imposed restrictions and prohibits them from pursuing natural remedies. Laws prevent these women from probing neighbours' lands in search of the shrubs and bushes that could be used as repellents or for medicines. As the studies by Shiva (2000) among Indian women show, women are environmentally friendly; they will not cut down shrubs and bushes or fell trees. They will nurture what nature has provided.

For Embu rural women, the yield from their farms has reduced considerably owing to the lack of crop rotation and the overuse of the land. In addition, coffee, tea, and pyrethrum cultivation has robbed many families of plots for growing food for home consumption. Kenya's plant diversity often becomes a nuisance during weeding time. Some plants grow freely and are an added burden for people who have no knowledge of their value. However, for those who do know how the plants can be used for preservatives, it is a blessing whenever they are found growing in their *shamba*. Wachiuma makes this point: "I always tell my children not to complain when they find these weeds in their plots. I have taught these children how to prepare these repellents, but they never listen to me. They tell me that these methods are too backward and old-fashioned." There are slight variations in repellent preparation. According to Wachiuma, the procedure depends on the purpose. The plants, which are beginning to flower, are cut into pieces, soaked in a drum that is half filled with water, and left for five to ten days, except for the occasional stirring. After the fifth (or tenth) day the decomposed plants are removed and used as mulch for vegetables. The rest of the solution is strained or filtered, then diluted with soapy water, and sprayed on the vegetables. This solution is effective in repelling aphids, caterpillars, and flies. Similar steps are followed in preparing a solution from hot pepper, onions, or garlic. Ciarunji emphasized that when she preserves dry foods, she does not soak the herbs in water, cow dung, or ashes. Rather, she mixes the food with the preservatives by forming layers of dry food and the preservatives. As I listened to these instructions, I was amazed at the attention to detail. Once in a while these women would ask me whether I was following what they were saying, and I would nod. Just as there are variations in what these women use, there are also variations in how the repellents are used. Warue had this to say: "I cannot tell you the amount of marigold to put in your food. Nor can I tell you this is the right way to do it because the amount depends on the type of food you are preserving. For instance, when I store unshelled maize or millet, I make a bed of marigold for the crop, and then use more of the repellent as a cover. I use my own judgment ... I learnt all this by observing and imitating my mother." The women who used pesticides, however, found the procedure simple if they could read the instructions. Njura said: "When I use pesticide, the process is simple. I just mix the powder with the grain. The only problem with the use of pesticide is the fact that most of us cannot read the instructions."

The older women spoke with ease on the subject of indigenous preservatives but were hesitant to talk about new forms of food preservation. Frequently, they distance themselves from the practices because they consider them foreign and unfamiliar; the instructions are written in English or Kiswahili, and most of the women cannot read. In most instances the women have to depend on their husbands to read the instructions to them. Angelina confirmed that her husband, Danieli, read the instructions to her, and if he was not around, she sometimes got things wrong.

As this chapter illustrates, the history and current realities of food preservation reflect the challenges facing the future of indigenous knowledge in Embu communities. As the challenge is multifaceted, it calls for a multifaceted approach, including decolonization and the reconstruction of local identities among young Embu women.

5 Gender Relations, Decision Making, and Food Preferences

As we have already noticed, the entire process of food preparation, food preservation, organization, management, and the utilization of indigenous resources is wrapped in governmental, gender, generational, environmental, and language considerations. It is complex and involves decision making, ownership, and control of resources – factors that are sensitive subjects but which cannot be ignored. In order to obtain answers from the women, I had to devise a technique of asking questions indirectly. For instance, one of the questions I asked was, "If you had a problem, could you take some of your beans and sell them?" From the answers I received it was obvious that they did not want to disturb the status quo and preferred to leave things as they were. However, the older women felt that the social organization of the decision-making patterns had been disrupted. Cucu recalls:

> During my time all the members of the clan knew the process of decision making. Like circumcision of the girls or piercing of their ears, every mother of the girl called a council of women elders. Honey beer was made, taken to the girl's maternal uncles to seek permission for ear piercing. These days I see girls piercing their own ears with the help of their older sisters or cousins, mothers making secret arrangements about circumcision of their daughters ... everything has broken down ... women give birth and give names to their children. Children are no longer dedicated to Mwene Nyaga [Creator] ... as I said; men and women knew what decisions to make on their own and which ones they had to make with consultation. The question of the land was left to the men, or anything to do with community, and the women took care of everyday decisions.

From Cucu's narrative, the decision-making pattern was governed by indigenous rules and regulations. It strengthened family ties, enabled people to share available resources, and ensured the continuity of tradition. Cucu laments the breakdown of these modes of decision making in the face of progress or new technological innovations. My conclusion to the above statement is that nothing is static, and with time the women have embraced the changes that speak to them or to the needs of their children. In fact, roles and duties were silently scripted, and each family member knew what he or she was supposed to do at any time or event. Within the family the wives were in charge of the daily running of the house. According to Wachiuma: "My husband never told me what to do with food. He never went to the granary to see how much food was left. He did not know what was to be cooked and how it was to be cooked. I had to work out the portions for immediate consumption as well as for future use. During times of famine I would consult with my husband and let him know that the food supplies were running low, and also involve my co-wives, and then a decision would be made. We worked together."

This illustrates how the husbands and wives used to discuss issues and come to agreement. However, the same women confirmed that this pattern of decision making has changed; Embu women now leave decisions to their husbands and do not consult their co-wives, because each woman lives a separate life. Most of the women admitted that they have left decision making to their husbands in order to avoid misunderstandings. As a consequence the men now decide what and where to plant. After harvest they decide what portion is to be put aside for everyday consumption and what portion needs to be sold. In many instances, women may be facing financial problems but do not dare to sell any of the produce, because, as Kanini said, the food does not belong to them; they are only managers: "To avoid any problems I usually leave things for my husband. Everything belongs to my husband. Even when we have to plant, he has to decide what is to be planted, whether we could use a tractor, a plough, and after the harvest whether we could use pesticide to preserve the food. If he has no money for the tractor or plough, then I have to struggle with the *shamba* alone. I have to let my husband know the number of sacks we have for beans or maize."

One would have thought that with the advent of technological changes an average indigenous Embu woman would have enough breathing space concerning her rights to own property. However, this has not been the case. In spite of changes introduced in the new constitution (2010) that women can own property, there are still challenges to their implementation. This is not to say that women have folded their hands and are waiting for changes to happen to them; they are making sure that the changes speak to their needs. A good example is the passing of the Sexual Offences Bill in 2006. The brain behind this bill was a woman, Njoki Ndungu. According to Njoki Ndungu, the bill was the first legislation of its kind in Africa. It was also the first gender-related act to be passed by Kenyan parliament since independence in 1963. Previous attempts to legislate gender-related bills like the Equality Bill, the Family Protection (Domestic Violence) Bill, and the Affirmative Action Bill were thwarted by the male-dominated Kenyan parliament. Njoki Ndungu's action and the narratives of participants in my research reinforce the various arguments of other scholars (such as Boserup, Marx, and Mackintosh) that subjugation of women has been entrenched in our society for a long time.

Even though the women were not explicit in their responses, it was evident that they were dissatisfied with the status quo. For example, women spend most of their time looking after the family's resources, yet they cannot claim ownership of them. Wawira noted that she could not sell any food, even when cash was needed in an emergency situation: "I cannot sell any food from the store unless my husband knows about it. If there is an emergency and I need money, I prefer to borrow from my neighbours, and then when he comes home, I explain what happened. What really is my food is the cooked food. I can give it out or eat it without asking my husband first. Again, when the food is still in the *shamba*, I can prune green beans or green maize – not for sale – for cooking, and he will not mind that. I cannot sell anything without telling him." Alice, the owner of a cattle farm, cannot use money made from the sale of milk or any farm produce because her husband bought her the cows, he controls everything, and the proceeds from the sale of milk are his. When I asked her about the coffee and to whom it belongs, she told me that the coffee was registered in her husband's name. Unfortunately for Alice, because she does not have a child, the proceeds from the sale of milk and cows go towards the tuition fees and other expenses of her rivals' children. Interestingly, she saw nothing wrong with this and, in fact, thought I did not understand the intricacies of being a barren woman in a polygamous relationship. "I do not have children. If I don't work hard and contribute to the family, my husband will take me back to my parents. I do not want that to happen. Furthermore, I am happy here. I have a home and these cows," she explained.

Although Alice accepts the role of submissive acquiescence, Rwamba says that the wife must be two steps ahead of the husband when it comes to control and access to property. She believes that there is no need for a wife to explicitly assume a position of control; that privilege should be left to the man. However, when the need arises, the woman should sell the food stuff and inform the husband later. Rwamba said:

> My husband died many years ago. I am alone now, and my children live with their families; they do not live here with me. And even when everybody was here, I was the one who used to decide what was to be planted and where. If I relinquished that responsibility, it would have meant that I had no role in the home; furthermore, what does a man know? My husband always used to wake up when the sun was up and I had already left for the *shamba*, and soon after, he would leave to visit his friends or go to the market, and I would only see him in the evening. How would he therefore know anything to do with the grains, cereals, and fruits? It is common sense. My husband could never tell me what to plant in my *shamba*; he had his own *shamba*. He could not tell me how to manage the food or how to preserve it. I used to tell him what I intended to do. I had learnt the skills from my mother. "Listen, my child," [she would say,] "Of course you do not show your husband your 'true colours,' you do not confront him, you have to smarten up, let him know he is in charge; but you are in charge." A man is not the one in charge of the home, because if you ask him what the family will have for supper, he cannot tell you. If you ask him how much food is in the granary, he cannot give you correct information. He has to enquire about the food situation. You cannot wait for a man to make decisions for you, but you have to let him know everything you do.

Rwamba sees gender relations differently than Alice does. She thinks it is not right for women to give so much power to men when it comes to the decision making that affects the whole family. It is evident that Alice, as a woman without children, is afraid that any assertive behaviour on her part will jeopardize her marriage. There is also a generational factor. Older women have a voice in marital relationships and, therefore, are able to tolerate the final decision-making authority of their husbands. According to Cucu and others in her age group (eighty years and older), decision making was communally based. However, this has changed because of a breakdown in indigenous social values. The younger women seem to leave the decision-making process to their husbands. Although they can make certain decisions if their husbands are not around, they are careful not to go against the norm.

While listening to these women's stories, I detected a clear distinction between the younger and the older women regarding the concept of decision making. The older women think that the void created in kinship relations and the wider community has created a generation of women who find it easier to submit to their husbands for the sake of peace and harmony than to demand respect and recognition, which would put the family relationship into chaos and disorder.

Western Influence on Food-Consumption Patterns

Issues of the Western influence on food-consumption patterns cannot be ignored among Embu rural people. While most of the adult Embu women favour indigenous food because of its nutritional value, the younger generation has developed a fondness for fast or pre-cooked food. Owing to technological advancement, it is possible to find pre-cooked maize meals or packaged banana chips. The age disparity in food preference is partially explained when one recognizes both the age and the education gap. The older generation prefers the indigenous foods that take more time to prepare; according to these women, the food has a higher nutritional value when compared to fast and pre-cooked food such as white bread. The younger women appear to associate Western food such as rice, spaghetti, and white bread with progress, and the local food with backwardness and underdevelopment. For some of the younger women, fast foods and pizza are great symbols of "success." For instance, it will take only twenty minutes to prepare a rice dish, while it takes two to three hours to prepare a meal from dried maize or beans. The long hours of preparing local food serve as a major source of dissatisfaction among Embu women. Even for some of the older generation, if given a choice, they would prefer to prepare easy cooking food such as rice and spaghetti than to prepare the local food, which takes a lot of time and resources (firewood and water) to cook. However, these women were unanimous in their conclusion that fast food, unlike local food, cannot satisfy hunger. Ciarunji said:

> I prefer our indigenous food. When you eat it, it fills you up. It gives you energy. Again you can preserve it for two to three days, and even a week or more, without [it] going bad, but not anymore. I do not know why. The other thing, our indigenous food contains everything: maize, beans, potatoes, bananas, and vegetables. Our food gave people strength. These days, many families seem to be hungry all the time. The new food cannot

remain in the stomach for long. You give your husband rice or *gitoero* [mashed bananas and potatoes], and within an hour you see him yawning. If you feed him with our foods, he will not complain of hunger and he will not ask for food until evening. But, interestingly, my children and grandchildren do not like our indigenous food any more. They prefer to eat *cheveveve* [new food].

Using preservatives prevents food from being destroyed by pests and also prolongs its lifespan. When the younger Embu women refuse to use preservatives, it is not because they are opposed to change but because they can afford the high cost of the new pesticides. A woman like Cucu, who was nearly a hundred years old when I interviewed her, refused to use pesticide or even eat food preserved with it because she did not trust what it contained and the possible harm it could do to the body. Pesticides are supposed to kill only pests, but they also destroy useful organisms on the farm. The women felt that the chemicals in pesticides had residual effects on the human body and could make one susceptible to diseases and suffering. It is interesting to note that the older women were aware of the eventual harm of pesticides. Mama did not hide her reservations: "I do not like this powder; its dust is not good for your lungs ... I have told my children never to use it, and they keep on using it even when I prepare the ashes or cow dung or marigold for them ... Again, how do I know the amount [of pesticide] to put? I hear my children complaining that they cannot follow the instructions."

Formal education is blamed for creating a generation of learners who show little interest in the indigenous ways of knowing (Thiong'o 1985). Most women believe that the school system indoctrinates the youth during their formative years to disregard indigenous knowledge (L.T. Smith 1999). These women also hold the opinion that the youth who have not acquired sufficient education to enable them to acquire gainful employment are placed at a disadvantage. Consequently, they cannot cope with life in their own local environment nor in the city. For Rwamba, the issue is not formal education but the general orientation of each generation. Although she will not use pesticides for food preservation or feed her family with fast foods, she does not want her children to be like her, because they are from a different generation and the change has to be embraced and celebrated – not rejected because it is new. But she cautions against over-dependency on any particular practice and product: "Our days were good, and these days are good for you. I keep telling my age group that we must learn from our children and also teach them as well. That way, we would appreciate new things, and they would appreciate eating, growing, and preserving arrowroot, cassava, yams, and millet. When there is scarcity, we would not starve ... but then you get used to using sugar in your tea, using the fine maize flour ... well, it is good, but when these things are not there, you have many problems. That is why I like to depend on myself and on my hands."

Rwamba is very wise, and I admired her pragmatic response to the changing time. There is a lot that could be gleaned from her words. Over the years, many anti-colonial scholars have advocated for the inclusion of indigenous knowledge in the school curriculum (see Dei 2004; Thiong'o 1986). For these scholars, while the Western knowledge system is good and has something relevant to offer learners, such knowledge has come at the expense of local knowledge. The suggestive words of Rwamba can guide us to create multiple learning centres in the academy where both indigenous and Western knowledge can be taught. There is more to gain when indigenous ways of knowing are incorporated in the teaching curricula. Not only is indigenous knowledge an alternative to the Western knowledge system, but it also serves as oppositional knowledge to some of the values, cultures, and world views in the Western system of thought. Indigenous knowledge restores the historical agency of local people. The presence of indigenous knowledge and Western knowledge in the classroom will produce well-balanced learners who have sophisticated tools to address some of the emerging complex issues in human development in today's global world. Women's knowledge of nature and the environment and all its manifestations is extensive, yet it is ignored, underestimated, and undervalued. Planners and innovators of African development must become more conversant with the physical, social, and cultural mores of the communities they propose to help. They need to understand the family structures, the gender roles, and the decision-making processes in these communities. Planners have to be aware of what women are willing to give up without suffering pain and regret, and what they can integrate into without violating their natural laws. Essentially, then, women's involvement in food-processing activities can only be understood in relation to the *totality* of the factors that comprise their lives. To acknowledge less is to do these women a great disservice.

6 Indigenous Technology and the Influence of New Innovations

Kenya's stone age was characterized by tools consisting of hand-size pebbles and stone blocks, which were later refined to produce crude but usable tools for cutting, digging, and breaking. Evidence of these tools can be seen in Koobi, east of Lake Turkana, an area now occupied by Nilotic people. Other tools such as hand axes and cleavers have been found at Olorgesailie, Kariandusi, Kilombe, Isinya, Mtongwe, and Lake Turkana (Salim and Janmohamed 1989). The Neolithic period is important because some of the tools that are used presently by the Embu people – stone bowls and platters, grinding stones, and pottery and wooden vessels – evolved during that time. According to Wachiuma, the indigenous technologies common in most families these days are the grinding stone, mortar and pestle, *munduri* (a round cooking stick used for mashing food in an earthen pot), and *mwiko* (a wooden stick with a flat end). Zeleza's (1993) research confirms that products such as leather, baskets, and pottery were part of items needed for food processing among many African communities. He further noted that, except in the Embu communities, these items were generally made by women.

The introduction of new technology has made indigenous food-processing practices among Embu women into something that is outmoded. In fact, most scholars today view such practices as relics of the past. Consequently there is the argument that Third World countries and rural women need a "technological fix" or "appropriate" technology that will increase efficiency and output (Stamp 1992). Unfortunately most of the "appropriate" technologies are gender biased and do not meet the real needs of women, who are supposed to be the targeted "beneficiaries." This could be attributed to knowledge-production cycles, accepted forms of knowledge, and the marginalization of the "voiceless." A typical example to buttress this point is the case of firewood and water provision among indigenous women in the Embu community.

Firewood and water play essential roles in food-processing practices. Rural women rely mainly on firewood as a source of energy and on water for virtually all household chores. The dependency of most Third World countries on wood fuel for their local energy consumption is about 78.5 per cent (Stamp 1992, 60). However, firewood sources have diminished substantially owing to forest destruction, low rainfall, overgrazing, commercial woodcutting, and charcoal production. According to Shiva (2000), twelve million hectares of forests are eliminated worldwide each year for industrial purposes. At the current rate of destruction all tropical forests will have disappeared by 2050, along with the diversity of the life they support.[1] This will make the collection of firewood more challenging than it is now for women all over the world where firewood is a source of fuel for cooking and for warming houses. Embu women have to compete for the few shrubs and bushes with charcoal burners and paper mills, and collection of firewood has become a nightmare for many women. Thus, the need for a technological fix is necessary and very urgent. Unfortunately the planners who design and implement innovations – such as new technology that will replace the use of firewood as a source of energy among the Embu community – overlook the social structure and the organization of indigenous households.

Feminist research needs to assess the dynamics involved in the provision of firewood in order to gain a full understanding of rural women's needs. A space must be created for indigenous forms of knowledge that are missing in present theory with regard to the problem of deforestation. The issue of women and water is well documented, but what has not been studied is the way in which women perceive the recently introduced methods of providing water for home consumption. It has been common for women to travel great distances in search of water for drinking and washing. Some women reject piped water because of its taste or because of the indigenous beliefs concerning spirits that inhabit the underground (Wint-Bauer 1986). Most areas where piped water is collected lack the facilities for laundry, showering, or washing.[2] Family members have to travel to take advantage of these basic needs even when they have access to piped water. There were similar concerns among Embu women, and it was not an unusual sight to see dried-up taps in many homesteads where I carried out my research. I received different answers from different women. Some women refused to use the water because the pipeline passed through a graveyard; others felt that they could not trust the water; some had not paid the water bill for the previous months; others did not have the money to pay the connection fee to the authorities for the water to flow. In addition, some women preferred to get their water from the river because the piped water did not have washing facilities. Usually the riverbeds were lined with stones that were ideal for scrubbing and washing clothes.

According to Meden and Meyers, there is evidence from the fields of anthropology, archaeology, mythology, and primate ethnology that women have been the main gatherers, processors, and keepers of plant foods from the earliest times. Their technology for gathering, processing, and cultivating food included the domestication and improvement of all the world's major plant foods and irrigation techniques (Meden and Meyers 1986). As societies increased their dependence on cultivation for their diets, a trend evolved towards male domination. This characteristic of mechanization becoming male gendered is quite evident in Third World countries.

It was noted in my research that the preparation of sugar-cane beer has been influenced by a similar transformation in technology. Initially the women used home-made graters to grate the sugar cane, but these were replaced by a hand-driven sugar-cane mill (very common in the 1960s), which was then replaced by a motor-driven mill. The maize and sugar mills, whether hand or motor driven, now belong to men. In the past, men created indigenous technology, and women used it to add value to food. Unfortunately, owing to new technology, this process has been abandoned. According to Warue: "Men operate these machines; they know what to do when they break down. I have no problem with men using these machines. The flour made is cooked by women. We carry on our backs the juice produced from the sugar cane ... We assist each other ... not sure whether it is because we cannot handle the machines. Look at the tractors or the lorries; it is the men who drive them. Women drive cars, but this was not always the case. I think women are scared. They do not want to handle what is not familiar to them." Rwamba still remembers when women used to grate sugar cane and prepare brew and how men used to help them squeeze the juice from the grated mixture. She recalls how everybody was fascinated when the first motor-driven sugar-cane mill was introduced in the area. However, the brewing of local beer has since become a male responsibility, and all that is expected of women is that they carry sugar cane to the mills and transport the sugar-cane juice (on their backs) to their homes.

It must be noted that a lot of new technology has been introduced with the intent of easing women's workloads, such as biogas, solar, and improved charcoal (*jiko*) stoves; grinding motors; and piped water. However, a closer examination of some of these technologies shows them to be unsuitable in many cases. For example, the introduction of biogas as a cooking fuel did not take into consideration the conditions under which the majority of rural women live; most of them cannot afford the required cast-iron stoves, and their kitchens lack the ventilation necessary for biogas stoves (Wint-Bauer 1986). Stamp (1992) makes the point that "replacing the indigenous three-stone fireplace in each hut with a single stove for the family raises the question of where to locate the stove and how to allocate the cooking time." In a society such as the Embu community where polygamy is practised, this new technology (a single stove) is almost certain to fail. Although polygamous families share many things together, one thing that a woman in a polygamous relationship will not share with her rivals is her kitchen. The kitchen is supposed to be the place in which the women prepare their secretly kept recipes for their husband. The understanding is that food and sex are the two routes to the heart of a man. Thus, a woman who is skilful in cooking always stands a better chance of being favoured not only by her husband but also by her in-laws and her husband's friends who are occasionally invited to eat in the house. Therefore, when the kitchen is shared, her rival can steal her recipe and with it the advantage she may have from being an excellent cook. As a result, many women in polygamous relationships do not appreciate the idea of sharing a kitchen with their rivals. In addition, a woman may need the kitchen to prepare food for her children at the same time as her rival is also using it. Also to be considered is that the new stove comes with its new cookware. Indigenous cookware is cheap and easy to use, but new technology, besides being expensive, requires one to buy costly cookware.

Studies related to new stoves in Sudan, Kenya, and other parts of Africa indicate that stove programs fail to reduce fuel consumption or ease women's workloads. There is a mismatch between the actual needs of the rural women and the assumptions of the institutions and individuals designing and promoting such stoves (Ibrahim and Slot 1989; Johnson-Odim 1991). According to my findings, close to 90 per cent (155) of the Embu women still used the three-stone indigenous cooking facility,[3] and 5 per cent (9) combined the three-stone and a *jiko* – a modified local technology for cooking. The rest of the women used both the three-stone and trenches.[4] Solar, gas, and electric cookers are innovations that are neither affordable nor convenient for most rural families.

Another observation made among the Embu rural community is that families differ in their use of methods to light and warm their houses. Some use *karambira* (wick lamps made from recycled tins) for lighting, while others use kerosene lanterns, and the three-stone fire is often used for cooking, lighting, and warmth. Rural electricity is a luxury that many will probably not have before 2020. Wangeci observed:

> We like to have a lantern lamp to light our house, but then we cannot afford it. Most of the time we depend on the glows from the burning wood to see, and some other times, when I have a little money, I buy paraffin for the wick lamp. I still remember how difficult it was when I was going to school. If I did not complete my homework during the day, I would have to be prepared for punishment the following day. Every Member of Parliament we elect promises us free electricity. It is now thirty-five years since we attained our independence, and our children cannot study at night because we do not have the lighting facilities.

Alongside the frustration and criticism expressed above, many of the women I spoke to are in fact content to use what they have for cooking purposes. As Kanini said, "my cooking pots have served me well for many years. The *cuvurias* were given to me by my parents, and the earthen pot was bought for me by my mother-in-law. The earthen pots are delicate, and I do not allow my children to scoop food from them." The cooking containers are *cuvurias* (aluminium cookware) and earthen pots, while calabashes and metal containers are used to collect water. The women carry the calabashes or the metal water containers on their backs, supported by ropes hanging from their heads. Owing to long usage of this mode of carrying loads, the women have a permanent groove or indent on their heads.

Some of the Embu women recalled with nostalgia the indigenous means of storing food. Warue used to store her food in a *miruru*, noting that her husband used to hang maize cobs on trees. "When I was growing up, every homestead had a *miruru* ... The granaries were built during the period when Kenyans were fighting for their independence. I am not sure why the government made us build granaries. It could be due to the fact that we were living in villages, and it was necessary to get the food under lock and key to prevent thefts." It is clear that indigenous storage facilities have undergone some transformation in response to current changes in social conditions. The granary has become the most commonly used storage facility, but families who have no granary store their food in sisal baskets, sacks, or metal containers. According to Alice, "the food can be either put in sacks or poured on the floor which has been smeared with cow-dung, or placed on a sisal mat or canvas sheet."

Cucu recalls how she acquired her grinding stone, digging stick, and mortar and pestle: "Do you see all these? They were my husband's wedding presents ... the *miro* [long stick used for digging], *munduri* [round cooking stick used for mashing food in an earthen pot], *mwiko* [cooking spoon], mortar and pestle. And if a woman did not have a husband, the men of the community made these items for her. It is unfortunate that we have abandoned most of these items." Indigenous men used to work with women to make indigenous tools. Cucu's husband knew that she would require these items for food processing; hence, they were the ideal wedding gift. However, times have changed. If a woman cannot persuade her husband to make any of the necessary items, she will hire another person from the neighbourhood to make them for her. Although cooking spoons and earthen pots are commercially available, they are expensive for most of these rural women. Hoes, ploughs, and tractors have replaced digging sticks.

Although most of the older respondents did not object to new technology, they were concerned about the complete negation of indigenous technology. According to Cucu, "development is good, but then everything that was old should not be destroyed. We should try to keep some of our good old things, foods and tools." Embu women are also concerned about wholesale acceptance of new technology. Rwamba complained about environmental pollution and the destructive element seemingly inherent in the machinery that had been introduced to the community. Although the tractors and maize mill save time and are more efficient than the manually operated technologies, women cannot identify with them.

There is a *spiritual* aspect that new technologies lack. They are impersonal and have no intrinsic qualities beyond their uses. Indigenous technologies, made by the hands of either the men or the women, are personal, and the food is prepared by using them as well as touch, smell, and judgment. The women bring their *selves* to the preparation, knowing that what they are doing is for the family's health and sustenance. There is pleasure in the preparation, a giving, and a sense of achievement. Thus, we also see the intrinsic spiritual aspect that infuses food preparation.

In the use of new technologies Ciarunji felt that she could not identify with the process of adding value to food. She spoke of the disadvantages of using a tractor. When women agree to have their land ploughed by a tractor, they give up the handling of the soil to something foreign. The machines uproot any plants and interfere with soil composition, and, most important, the women lose the sense of sacredness that comes from working with nature. "The grinding stone is tiring and takes a lot of your time, and then you take only a day in a week, prepare gruel for your family that lasts a week or more ... Again, gruel or local brew were significant foods for marriage, circumcision, and baby-naming ceremonies. These were ceremonial foods, and when you cease to prepare them, you abandon your tradition" (Wangeci). Cucu did not consider the energy required in using indigenous technology to be a source of major problems compared to its significance. In her opinion, embracing innovation without understanding it is tantamount to displacing a significant aspect of an indigenous culture. Although new forms of foods have become part of the rural Embu diet, Cucu still believes that indigenous food has much more to offer than does the new food. "What we had was good. We had herbal tea growing behind our houses; the newly married woman ground the flour and prepared the gruel." She views indigenous technology as a source of unity within the community and feels that the new technologies have disturbed this, bringing individualism and destroying the fabric of society. Wawira, however, sees new technologies as a source of positive alternatives and a timely blessing: "I think all these were appropriate for my parents' era. The grinding stone, mortar and pestle now have alternatives."

Admittedly these women do have choices, but to take advantage of these choices depends on a family's financial capabilities. The research noted that women who committed to using the new technology faced serious constraints if they did not have the financial resources. It was evident that the younger generation who had not acquired the skills and knowledge to use indigenous technology were placed at a disadvantage when they could not afford to purchase new technological equipment.

Alice did not master indigenous skills although she was familiar with indigenous technology by observing her mother. She preferred the new technology: "I never learnt how to use a grinding stone or a mortar and pestle, but I used to observe when my mother was grinding maize and I would try to imitate her. I was not very keen to learn how to use them, and I spent most of my early years in school. Once in a while, I grind millet or maize with the stone." Kanyiva, a woman of the younger generation, explained that she neither owned any of the utensils common to indigenous technology nor intended to own any, because they were backward and embarrassing to use. Even though she conceded that new technologies were expensive, she still preferred them to the indigenous ones. "That would be very backward for me. If I had the money, I would have a *jiko* or a gas cooker. I would also buy packaged maize flour, but everything is so expensive. A few years ago a packet of maize flour was twenty shillings, and this year it is almost a hundred shillings. I have learnt to substitute, and instead of using packaged flour, I take maize to the maize mill if I have money." Obviously, Kanyiva and Alice, who are exposed to colonial schooling, regard indigenous technological practices as old fashioned and embarrassing. Even as the older generation is aging, the younger women are unwilling to acquire these knowledges. The future of indigenous knowledges is bleak unless efforts are made to document them.

In addition, the older women also thought that the men had lost the skills of making tools because they had come to rely on formal education. The women challenged the value of this education and insisted that the "educated" contributed to the destruction of the environment. Some younger women thought that the new technology created a dependency situation while others thought that it provided choices and alternatives. As Wekiya (1992) states: "Technology is not only hardware. It also involves skills, expertise, techniques, and organization. In fact, the whole body of knowledge is connected with a production process. How then can women, holders of that knowledge, be left behind when planning or making policies or designing technologies? We say women should always be included at all stages of planning, decision making, and in the designing of machines; this will save time and money."

There are many complexities inherent in the conflict between new and indigenous technologies. Each technology has its adherents. Generational views often differ, financial capacity is a major factor, and societal or community attitudes are potential influences. However, one fact is indeed clear: tradition is threatened, indigenous technologies are endangered, and their future is uncertain.

7 Removing the Margins: Including Indigenous Women's Voices in Knowledge Production

Knowledge production is not an exercise exclusive to academia. Unfortunately, within Western knowledge discourse one is assumed to have acquired legitimate knowledge only when it has been received in a formal classroom setting. This concept often causes educated researchers to disregard indigenous knowledges. In most cases, research on indigenous peoples is patronizing, often depicting their culture, knowledge, values, and world views as crude, unlearned, and unproductive. As a result, custodians of indigenous knowledge are reluctant to openly share what they know, particularly when the researcher operates from a Western or Eurocentric bias.

The Responsibilities of a Researcher

During my initial meeting with Cucu I sensed some mistrust and scepticism as to whether my interest in indigenous knowledge was genuine. In fact, Rwamba directly questioned my sincerity: "How will I know what I have taught you has been mastered? You young people are here today and the next minute you have flown like birds, leaving behind the skills and knowledge imparted to you by us. How will I know what I tell you will be taken seriously and will not be wasted?" Her question is legitimate. All too frequently, Western anthropologists and scientists have either misrepresented local knowledges or appropriated them without attributing recognition to those from whom they were acquired. Ghanaian literary writer Ama Ataa Aidoo has reiterated the concerns like those from Rwamba when she problematizes the misrepresentation of African peoples and their cultures in numerous academic works: "Africans have been the subjects of consistent and bewildering pseudo-scholarship, always aimed at proving they are inferior human beings. Even when there is genuine knowledge it [is] handled perniciously by anthropologists and social engineers, cranial and brain-size scientists, sundry bell-curvers, doomsday, medical and other experts" (Aidoo 1998). In spite of this, local women are willing to share their knowledges once the researcher has overcome the "threshold crossing" ritual by essentially establishing identity and sincerity through lineage and legacy. Threshold crossing is of paramount importance in creating rapport and acceptance between the learner and the instructor. For the women to perform the ritual of acceptance, they have to be convinced that the outsider has a genuine desire and interest in knowing the various aspects of not only their past but also their everyday realities.

Some time ago Cashman (1991) reminded us that focusing on the nature and origin of women's knowledge is a political act. Acknowledging and documenting this knowledge as a resource is equivalent to redistributing power. However, the knowledge possessed by women on food issues has generally been undocumented. Overlooking this valuable resource means that important knowledge about survival strategies may be lost. Historically, women's knowledge has been trivialized. Further, as soon as any knowledge acquires importance, it becomes appropriated. Maina and Murray (1993, 4) write:

> Throughout human history, men for various reasons have appropriated women's knowledge. Health is one of those spheres where women's knowledge and practices have been usurped and used by [the West] to further their own interests ... Our fore-mothers were the first healers ... [yet] as medicine and healing became a source of social influence and economic power, [the West once again has] appropriated all acclaim and barely acknowledges women's role as knowers in the creation of the healing process. The same can be said of women's knowledge about food and food processing. While [the West] has looked down on women's knowledge as it relates to reproductive activities, they [will/did] not miss the opportunity to appropriate and exploit such knowledge when it served their interests. A clear example of this is in the transformation from domestic worker/cook to chef when women's cooking skills and knowledge are appropriated and relocated into the public sphere. Being a chef implies enormous status and prestige.

It is evident that any effort to validate and legitimize local knowledges and the culturally based capabilities of women's food-processing technologies can be a source of empowerment not only for the women but also for their local communities. As we examine the nuances, both implicit and explicit, that pervade the realities of the rural Embu woman, we have to confront the relational collocation between indigenous education and the social politics of gender. According to Nasimiyu (1997, 283), among the Luyia of western Kenya at the "beginning of the twentieth century, the Luyia family was an economically self-sufficient unit. The wife and husband, children and other dependents contributed to the maintenance of the family group by performing tasks allocated within the household through an indigenous gender division of labour. Among the Luyia, land was never owned in the western sense of the word. In fact, the concept of ownership with reference to land was unknown. Land was a communal property." Nasimiyu explains that land use and administration were vested in clan elders, who were usually male. However, women's use of land was nevertheless guaranteed within this patriarchal system. Pre-colonial communal systems recognized the crucial contributions of women in food production. Thus, they gave women economic security and stability in land-use rights. However, this state of affairs changed drastically during colonial and post-colonial eras. Owing to the introduction of different forms of land ownership, many women lost the use of the clan land. Regarding laws of inheritance, Nasimiyu (1997, 290) states: "Property allocated to individual houses was protected by customary law which also recognized women's usufruct rights in land and cattle. There, while inheritance was patrilineal, specific rights in the patrimony were transmitted through women, whose status as wives was important in determining the inheritance of their sons. This system of inheritance encouraged subdivision of land. The colonial officials opposed this system, because it increased fragmentation and created uneconomical land units."

Nasimiyu (1997) also describes the changes in the land-tenure system and their implication for women. She states that the people of Kenya were dispossessed of much of their land through a series of measures instituted by the British colonial government between 1897 and 1926 (Sorrenson 1968; Wolff 1974). From 1897, European settlers could secure a ninety-nine-year lease on crown lands (Breen 1976; Sorrenson 1968). In 1901, crown lands were defined as those not being cultivated by Africans (Nasimiyu 1997, 291). According to Nasimiyu (1997, 292), these changes in the land-tenure system affected women: "As land became scarcer, patriarchal structures already in place in the pre-colonial period protected men rather than women. As individual control over land increased and costs rose, many women lost access to the land." Nasimiyu also mentions a few unique cases in which women were able to acquire land title deeds. The changes in the land-tenure system provided an indirect opportunity for women to purchase and own land in their own right (294). Women and children also continued to provide the labour needed for the production of cash crops such as maize and coffee, which were marketed through cooperative societies (294).

It is one thing to listen to people's stories but quite another thing to make sense of them. From the older women I heard their fading past; from the younger women I heard their frustration at being at the crossroads. I listened to the older women with incredulity, dazzled by their vast knowledge of indigenous healing practices and the social, political, and economic practices that held indigenous structures intact. I was also impressed with how the younger women combined several chores and executed each of them efficiently. Language, both verbal and non-verbal, is central in knowledge acquisition. These women used proverbs, idioms, songs, and wise sayings as their means of communicating events of the past. The myriad forms of transmitting knowledge and understanding can be compared to the spokes of a wheel that are attached to the hub; the hub in this instance is indigenous knowledge, and the spokes the many ways of bringing order and synthesis. All are valid; all are connected. There is wholeness. Various rules prevail in conversation. For example, to indicate that one is participating and listening, one has to continually say *uhmu*. A young person cannot ask an elder a direct question, and asking older people their age or name is considered disrespectful. I recall how furious Cucu was when I asked her age. I was firmly chastised: "Children of these days have no respect for their elders. My own husband never asked me my age. Didn't your mother tell you that it was not appropriate to ask people of their age?"

During my research I discovered that one way to know a woman's estimated age was by checking her national identity card. In most cases the age written on these cards is incorrect. To help establish age, I would ask the respondent to recall important social or political events that had taken place during their lives. Their reference to historical events such as the advent of the Europeans, the First World War, famine, droughts, or circumcision enabled me to approximate their ages. Through this procedure I also learned about most aspects of their communities. To approximate Cucu's age, for example, I asked about her earliest remembrance. "I can still remember when these *Wachungu* [white people] came. When they saw Kirinyaga [Mount Kenya], they were taken aback by the mountain with a white top, but they could not pronounce its name, and called it *Kii-nyaa*.[1] My child, everybody was fascinated by these people; their feet had no toes, they ate fire, and they wore clothes that were not like ours. It was soon after this that I got circumcised."[2]

From Cucu's recollections I was able to approximate her age at 106 years or more. This means of information retrieval was common among the older women who applied the theory of association. Language use was also highly important, especially when the women made references to the past. When they spoke of "several moons," they were referring to a number of seasons. The sun also played an important role. Checking the sun's position allowed them to determine how much more daylight they had to complete their daily chores. Their language indicated their close relation with nature's cycles. Knowing the name of one's tribe or clan was not enough as far as these women were concerned; one had to know several generations of one's family tree. In this way, lineage was established, and because this was a small community, it was ultimately revealed that all of us were connected at some branch of the family tree. After ancestry had been established, the narrative began, generally following a pattern of questions such as, "Whose daughter did you say you were?" "What is your clan?" "What about your mother's clan?"

Once the bond had been established, I knew that the elders could question my opinion and understanding of any issue. I had become their grandchild, their daughter, or sister. However, I was at a crossroads, trying to execute an academic exercise while simultaneously re-establishing my Embu identity. Cucu placed me in the centre as a challenge. She could clearly see that I was in the middle of various discourses, and everything was gravitating towards the centre where I stood overwhelmed by her knowledge. My sincerity and patience in going through the ritual of crossing the threshold earned me the trust that was required of a pupil.

Indigenous Knowledge and Rites of Passage for Young Women

The purpose of a learning process is to expand the learner's mind on every aspect of life including the socio-economic realities of a society. In indigenous society, learning embraced every facet of life and was not isolated from food preparation, preservation, or consumption. It was during these various stages that children learned about their culture, indigenous beliefs, and customs. Consequently, it was impossible to know when instruction of the young ones in food preparation actually began. I could not therefore separate from the indigenous rites of passage what I learned from the women in terms of food. I had accepted being a pupil and learning whatever I could while I was with these women. It is therefore important to contextualize the learning process in a particular indigenous society within the context of my research and not to view this process as a separate research project. It was not unusual to hear a mother repeat an idiom or a proverb during her domestic or farm work. It was quiet in order to have grandmothers tell the same stories over and over again in the evening while the food was being prepared for dinner. I was quick to note that storytelling or memorization of idioms and proverbs protected the knowledge necessary for a society's survival. It is unfortunate that oral history has been subjected to great criticism. I have chosen only a few perspectives to illustrate the learning processes among the Embu. These areas include indigenous education (inculcation of social skills), discipline, health, healing, and circumcision.

Every society, no matter its level of economic development, has some form of purposeful education. Defined in its broadest sense, education is a conscious attempt to help people live in their society and participate fully and effectively in its organization in order to ensure their continued existence.[3] Education is normative and based on the values of each society. Education implies that something worthwhile is being or has been intentionally transmitted in a morally acceptable manner. Therefore, it would be a contradiction in logic to say that a person has been educated but has in no way changed for the better or that education is worth nothing (Peters 1966). Indigenous education is about inculcating what a given society considers as valuable and worthwhile to learners. Indigenous Embu, like any other groups, have an education system based on the philosophy of their traditions. The Embu believe that the nature of reality (*ontology*) is based on the assumption that all elements of the universe are derived from similar substances and are in essence spiritual. They insist that for one to understand the reality of life, one needs a complete or holistic view of society. The Embu recognize the interdependency of all peoples and, by extension, that individual existence is only meaningful in relation to the community of which she or he is a part. Thus, a person's success story is meaningless to the Embu community if it is not linked to the members of his or her family and community. Again, the Embu believe that the study of reality (*epistemology*) should not be based on only one way, because there are multiple ways of knowing reality. Knowledge accumulated through emotions, dreams, intuition, and visions should be recognized for its authentic means of understanding or studying the reality. For Embu women, practice and experience form the contextual basis of producing knowledge. Hence, survival should always go hand in hand with knowledge. In this sense, experience should be allowed to teach knowledge. This means that those who are fortunate to have lived long in a community (the elders) should become the source of knowledge for the younger generation. The concept of rights and responsibilities is something that is cherished worldwide by all societies. Whereas other societies place more emphasis on rights, the Embu community thinks that responsibility should be encouraged more than rights. Thus, the community rewards actions that are geared towards the good of the community rather than the good of the individual. The society encourages peaceful coexistence with nature rather than total control or dominion over nature. These philosophical values serve as a guide in formulating and developing the education system among the Embu community.

The Embu in this study had been exposed to both indigenous and formal education. Until more recently, the purpose of indigenous education within Embu society was to train the youth for adulthood. Children were taught their social, economic, and political roles along with their rights and obligations. The methods of instruction encompassed oral narratives (in many forms, as outlined earlier), observation, and participation. The various rites of passage were the final 'institutions' of learning. The piercing of the ears of both boys and girls marked the transition from childhood to boyhood or girlhood. Before the piercing, the boys had been placed under the guidance of their fathers, while the girls had been left to prepare for their roles as women through role playing, imitation, and observation (Kenyatta 1965). Studies by Kenyatta (1965) and Sifuna (1990) reveal the steps that girls had to go through in preparation for their roles as future wives and mothers. As for the boys, their fathers taught them how to prepare digging sticks and learn the names of various plants and roots and their uses, particularly, as antidotes for insect or snake bites. Mothers used lullabies as an instruction method. According to Kenyatta (1965), the whole history and tradition of the family was embodied in these lullabies, and by hearing them daily, the children would assimilate this early teaching without strain.

During my fieldwork the singing of lullabies to babies was not common, especially among the younger women. Although the older women sing to their grandchildren, it is not done as frequently as it once was.

These women lament the loss but can do little to rectify the situation. The question of lullabies cannot be discussed intelligently without an understanding of the essence of indigenous ways of knowing or the place of indigenous education among Embu rural women. As Kojo B. Maison (2007, 27–8) argues, "any form of education is situated within a cultural environment and exists as a tool of culture ... The sole purpose of education is the intergenerational transmission of the process ... Therefore any real education for any people should be factored into the people's ontology, cosmology and axiology." The purpose of lullabies, therefore, lies not in singing to a child strapped on someone's back but in understanding the significance of these songs, because, as Maison advances, one of the goals of indigenous forms of knowledge transmission is to "culture a person or child into the community" (28). In the pre-colonial Embu society significant stages in one's life were marked by a special ceremony (*mambura*). The most celebrated stages were birth, the piercing of a girl's ears, circumcision of both boys and girls, and marriage. During these *mamburas* there would be drinking, eating, dancing, rejoicing, and teaching. Unfortunately most of the rites are no longer observed, because they have been made illegal, they have lost significance, or economic hardship prohibits ceremonial celebrations.

It is evident that there has been a breakdown in the social fabric of Embu's indigenous organizational structure. Older women complained that the youth have lost respect for their elders. According to these women, a nation whose people do not have good standing or have lost the social consciousness cannot remain intact or cohesive. Indigenous education was based on principles of collective responsibility, and the importance of community cohesiveness was developed in the youth through various rites of passage. Disciplining children was part of the learning process and depended on their age and gender. Before circumcision both parents could exercise discipline, but the responsibility was left more to the women than to the men. In other words, regardless of whether or not they were the biological parents, the "mothers," aunties, and grandmothers had a duty to correct the young and give them a spanking on occasion. After puberty or circumcision the boys became the responsibility of the men, and the girls the responsibility of the women in the homestead.

This pattern has changed. Grandparents, aunts, and uncles no longer have the authority over children that was once traditionally accepted. Young Embu girls who were exposed to Western education have embraced some of the Victorian notions of gender and domesticity. For instance, some of the girls who went to formal schools were taught several skills such as home economics and needlework to prepare them for their expected future roles in nurturance and housewifery. Although this knowledge alone cannot be responsible for some of the drastic changes among young Embu women, it definitely contributed to the creation of new generations who had different attitudes towards some of the local and indigenous knowledge about food preservation. There appears to be resentment, resistance, and a breakdown in communication between the older generations and the new generations. There is dislocation between young and old, each viewing the other as ignorant. There is rupture as the new social structures have become polarized. Older women have little or no say in shaping the lives of the future generation and are ignored when they try to offer advice. Structures that once held families and community together have largely been shunted into irrelevance. However, there remain other issues that call for consideration. For instance, there is currently a concerted effort to reintroduce the indigenous rites of passage for adolescent girls. A group of women has initiated a ceremonial rite equated with the different stages of growing up in Kenya. For example, circumcision practices were previous associated with puberty rites; according to a recent report, a week-long celebration (without circumcision) is held during which girls are given sex education, life skills, and childcare classes. The girls are made aware of their cultural traditions as they celebrate their passage into adolescence. People are beginning to accept the significance of these rites of passage because they are centred on the indigenous teachings and socialization that accompany the week-long ceremony. To date, approximately one thousand girls have experienced the new ceremonial rites of passage into adulthood.

Indigenous Health Practices and Food Processing

It is difficult to separate the issue of indigenous health practices from food processing. Older women spoke of various roots, leaves, and herbs that can be used either as a health drink or as treatment of an ailment. The notion of indigenous herbs broadens the issue of indigenous knowledge and the environment. Western medicine, like education and Christianity, was geared to serve European interests. After independence, however, medical facilities were made available to everyone regardless of race or religion. Although this study does not focus on health facilities, it is appropriate to indicate the state of such facilities in Kenya and their accessibility for rural populations.

The poverty conditions of African countries are often noted through the indicators of life expectancy – disease, health conditions, and the availability of basic amenities such as water and housing. There have been some improvements in the health status of Kenyans following independence. In the 1970s, 1980s, 1990s, and 2000s, two-thirds of the health budget went into curative care, typified by the construction, administration, and maintenance of large medical facilities. During the same periods, however, rural health services received only 8.9 per cent of the health budget, and preventive health – immunization against communicable disease, attention to adequate nutrition, public health, and health education – received 6.7 per cent.[4] While emphasis has been on curative care, major causes of mortality are ill health and diseases that can be prevented through community actions and improvement of conditions outside medical facilities.[5] In 1980, 60 per cent of the total reported deaths were found to be from preventable diseases. During the same year, 33 per cent of children's deaths were directly related to malnutrition (Ahlberg 1991).

In spite of the increase in the number of medical facilities and personnel, the effectiveness of medical care is limited by the nature of its orientation and structure. Although clinics in rural areas are within the reach of the people, they are generally understaffed and in most instances do not have the necessary drugs. Significant numbers of the people in general, and specifically those in rural locations, are forced to continue using indigenous medicines. This state of affairs is evident among the women interviewed. Fifty per cent used indigenous herbs to treat maladies, and 34 per cent combined both Western medicine and indigenous herbs. Only 3 per cent did not rely on any of the indigenous medicines to treat either their own ailments or those of their children. From statistical data in case studies by Simwogere (1992), Wekiya (1992), and Labai (1992), it is evident that food processing cannot be studied in isolation.[6] The practice has to be examined in relation to a myriad of family, community, and government factors. Only then can one appreciate the interdependency involved. In addition, it is critical that there be a continuous effort to wrestle local knowledges from the margin and bring them closer to the centre of knowledge production. This may be achieved through curriculum design in which children are introduced to indigenous knowledge systems during their formative years (from kindergarten to grade 12). Internal structures must be constituted to rescue indigenous practices from extinction.

While some traditions may seem less than ideal when evaluated against a capitalist or Western view, many indigenous traditions serve to strengthen the bond between and within families and, by extension, their communities. The emancipation of African women will begin when their voices are given the respect and dignity afforded them by past generations. It is these women who created, create, and perpetuate indigenous knowledge of food-processing technologies – a key area that deserves recognition and respect.

8 Contesting Knowledge: Some Concluding Thoughts

Within the overlapping circles of knowledge are questions about the credibility of the generally accepted voices that frame knowledge. Francis B. Nyamnjoh (2004) expressed his reservation about Western constructs of "valid" knowledge, particularly when they are compared to indigenous epistemologies of the African continent. He centred his criticism on the basis that Western constructs of knowledge tend to exclude anything that is not considered to have been established in a rational, objective manner. Thus any form of knowing that cannot be expressed in behaviourist terms is discarded as unreal, metaphysical, irrational, subjective, and in some cases primitive. I propose that indigenous ways of knowing "the self" exist within a world subject to flux. These knowledge forms reunify or reconcile a learner to his or her world. Indigenous knowledges, therefore, are the source of all teachings through which caring and feelings survive the tensions of living within contexts of flux, paradox, and contention. They respect the pull of dualism and conciliate opposing forces. In the realms of flux and paradox, "truthing" is a practice that enables a person to know the spirit in every relationship, and the development of these ways of knowing leads to freedom of consciousness and solidarity with the natural world.

In fact, in African systems of thought, knowledges have been constructed to validate and legitimate the pluralist way of knowing. In other words, indigenous ways of knowing accept and validate multiple ways of knowing the physical and metaphysical, the real and unreal, the rational and irrational, the objective and subjective, the natural and spiritual, and finally, science and superstition. In reality, indigenous knowledges do not restrict the arena of production, validation, and distribution of knowledges to any specific areas as do Western or conventional ways of knowing. Intuitions, dreams, visions, proverbs, oral narratives, songs, fables, myths, and superstitions are all validated as legitimate forms of knowing. Indigenous knowledges are produced in homes, communities, and environments. This is aptly pertinent among the Embu rural women to whom the practice of food processing is a site of theorizing culturally and traditionally informed pedagogies. Unfortunately these ways of accumulating knowledge are not considered legitimate in conventional Western classrooms. I have observed that Western discourse has justified the neocolonial agenda, which remains deeply embedded in systems of education that influence current ways of thinking among Embu rural women. Colonialism, I believe, began as an idea that became a philosophy, a creed, and a way of life. This meant that people's land and their physical and mental capacities should be taken away from them through forced or persuasive indoctrination that would advance this exploitative agenda.

In a different context, indigenous scholar Smith (1999) has posited that Western knowledge and culture has placed itself as pivotal to civilization and knowledge legitimacy and that imperialism sanctioned the rule or control of non-Western nations and cultures. Similarly, Semali and Kincheloe (1999) have argued that the tyranny of Western epistemology decrees that the reality worth talking about at the centre of knowledge production should be the one sanctioned by Cartesian science and behaviourist knowledge systems. It is no wonder that what is considered legitimate knowledge is limited to Eurocentric and androcentric power blocs. It is obvious that this framework, used as the benchmark by which the production of non-Western civilizations was measured, influenced late-seventeenth-century Europeans and underpinned their condescension towards "primitive" knowledges of other cultures. Such perceived primitivism justified the "civilizing" efforts of the "white man" and the pedagogical dynamics embedded in the concept.[1]

Confronted by this enormous conceit, scholars of decolonization have suggested that in order for African peoples to liberate themselves from the colonial-based exclusivity on knowledge validity, they need to revisit their creative initiatives in history, cultures, values, and world views.[2] A thrust towards bringing the indigenous voices of rural Kenyan women from the margin to the centre of knowledge production is essential for their liberation from the quagmire of self-denigration imposed on them through the colonial domination of thought, belief, and actions. As noted by Semali and Kincheloe (1999), Shiva has observed that colonial history has constantly labelled those non-Western peoples (African, Asian, and Aboriginal) whose knowledges have been systematically usurped and negated as being ignorant, primitive, and inferior. In addition, their knowledge systems are viewed as less valuable and/or irrelevant in the contemporary world.[3] According to Semali and Kincheloe (1999), the term *indigenous* and the concept of *Indigenous Knowledges* have often been associated with Western understanding (and fetishization) of primitive and wild. The Western (Eurocentric) world has deftly divided humanity into "civilized" and "uncivilized," creating an adversarial ethos wherein it has taken upon itself the burden of "civilizing primitive peoples *for their own good.*" History confirms that the good is more often attributed to the conqueror, the oppressor, the imperialist, the colonialist. Indigenous knowledges have received no recognition, and they are ridiculed, demonized, and assigned to the margins of knowledge production.

My research findings among Embu rural women in Kenya suggest that valid knowledge should be viewed in a cultural context, a context that respects form and purpose. These women knew the right language to use when addressing issues related to the land. They knew the appropriate words to appease the ancestors buried in that land. After observing different methods of food processing and preservation, I immediately recognized that to the uninformed and biased Western mind the methods and indigenous technologies would be quickly classified as primitive. This deprecatory labelling of cultures whose traditions and practices do not conform to the Eurocentric world view of what is acceptable and valid must be challenged. But the labelling also contributes to something considerably more insidious: a psychological and spiritual dissonance engendered in those who are the targets of noxious characterizations. An example of this is captured in the *Song of Lawino*, a poem by the Ugandan writer Okot p'Bitek (1995) who echoes these sentiments through Lawino. Lawino questions the Acholi people's having to pray to foreign ancestors – such as Joseph, the father of Jesus, or some of Jesus's disciples such as Peter and Luke – and not to Hunchback (God), the Acholi god, to intercede for them. She wonders why her husband says, "It is stupid superstition / To pray to our ancestors / To avert [misfortunes]."

Ogot p'Bitek's words highlight a lingering problem, which is told through the words of Lawino, an indigenous African woman whose marriage is on the verge of dissolution because her husband, Ochol, a product of Makerere University of Uganda, claims she is not educated enough to be his wife. Ochol uses every opportunity to denigrate and belittle his indigenous customs, values, and world views, as well as his wife, who is not willing to discard these traditions. For instance, he does not want his wife to wear the toe of a rat, the horn of a rhinoceros, or the jawbone of an alligator, and he once beat her up for wearing them. Although Ochol unhesitatingly criticizes indigenous practices as primitive, uncivilized, and fetishized, he readily endorses and accepts similar practices in Christianity as superior. Ochol wears a crucifix on his neck, and all his daughters wear rosaries, but he does not want his wife to wear a traditional elephant tail around her neck.

Legitimate questions arise regarding the way in which the knowledge industry defines and constructs myths, superstitions, and knowledges that are construed as "primitive." It is important to note that the ideas and practices that the West accepts as credible will often, and surprisingly, be dismissed as superstition, myth, and primitiveness if they occur in indigenous communities. As noted in the *Songs of Lawino*, Ochol, the converted Christian, cherishes the wearing and use of crucifixion and rosary, yet abhors indigenous people who wear talismans. Within the Western context, prayer to Mary, a Christian saint, or God is lauded, yet indigenous libation through ancestors to the supreme deity is ridiculed. While Western scholars acknowledge and sometime even practise religion, albeit not openly in the classroom, they are quick to dismiss and offer little intellectual sympathy when local people practise their own indigenous religion. The Western mindset takes unto itself the determining of what is right and wrong, proper and improper, valid and invalid, civilized and primitive. Thus, we can see that the constructs are derived from an assumption that the "other" is inferior. To understand the "other," we need to examine the consciousness that has generated this dual classification. For instance, Maison (2007) argues that "culturally literate individuals, known as the Indigenous Africans, are processed through an education whose conscious matrix is situated within an indigenous culture. It is such an indigenously processed person who has come to be perceived as 'primitive' and 'backward' by those who have received formal education" (29). Maison (2007) further states that the contemporary school system in Africa is "situated in the consciousness matrix of Europe and therefore serves as an institution to systematically deny Africa and the African of his/her Africaness ... This consciousness matrix has created the 'civilized' or 'modern' or 'progressive' Africans" (30).

The claim that Western knowledge holds the only keys to understanding the universe and all that is in it must be refuted and interrogated in both formal classrooms and centres of knowledge production. Knowledge is neither static nor restricted to one specific culture.

Within Western science, research in every field of learning has disproved many cherished beliefs and has caused mental confusion in many African intellectuals who believe that colonization brought positive changes into Africa. Maison, however, explains that changes could have been introduced to Africa without "going through the mill of colonialism" (31). Once, the Western mind believed that the Earth was flat. Although, interestingly, there remain those committed to that belief, science has proved otherwise. Knowledge is composed of building blocks that gradually advance our understanding. New discoveries change our views of the universe. The producers, validators, and distributors of knowledge must revise their narrow definitions of what constitute the building blocks and be willing to provide legitimate space for those who articulate differing concepts and theories. But non-Westerners who have attempted to bring new ideas, theories, or cultural world views that run counter to Western forms and ways of knowing are generally and frequently ignored. A lack of understanding of indigenous peoples' relationship with the environment in all its myriad manifestations – both the seen and the unseen – should not be a reason to disavow the validity of indigenous interpretations. Dei (2000b) has often posited that the most dangerous of all illusions is the presumption that one's reality is the only one worth promoting. Albert Einstein (1951), one of the world's most renowned Western scientists, once remarked that "we should be on our guard not to overestimate science and scientific methods when it is a question of human problems, and we should not assume that experts are the only ones who have a right to express themselves on questions affecting the organization of society." There is no revelation in Einstein's statement of what constitutes an expert. Applying the above statement to the Embu women in Kenya, we should thus recognize that they have their own ways and sites of producing knowledge – ways and sites that differ from those vaunted in the West and which are no less valid.

Historical and anthropological accounts by early European travellers, missionaries, explorers, and colonizers portrayed indigenous African women as savages requiring civilization. These views were promoted through Western religious concepts and Victorian ideals and ideas. It was suggested that women would be far more 'human' if they were taught skills such as baking, preparing afternoon teas, and using basic hygiene. The imposition of Victorian values disregarded the on-site realities of the women involved and failed to account for the fact that African women were expected to spend their time and energy fending for their families – unlike privileged Western women who were fortunate to have ladies in waiting. Aidoo (1998) has discussed how the contemporary African woman is a creation of historical and current forces that are simultaneously internally generated and externally induced from social structures and foreign forces. The image of the African woman in the Western mind was set, and this image is concisely described by Aidoo as a construction of a woman who is breeding too many children that she cannot take care of; a woman who may expect others to care for her children; and a woman who, along with her children, is hungry. Aidoo goes on to describe a woman whose children have flies buzzing around their faces and who has a permanent begging bowl in her hand (1998). Current educational practices, media imaging, and capitalist ideology maintain persistent hegemonic practices of neocolonization.[4] There is evidence, therefore, that neocolonial tactics have changed and the destruction of other cultures or the appropriation of indigenous knowledges is no longer overt. Elsewhere I have made reference to an African indigenous woman's statue erected at the gates of a multinational company that processes food. The statue depicting a woman grinding corn is a misrepresentation of indigenous Embu women because the grinding-of-corn posture suggests that the food behind the closed gates is being processed in a way that is similar to that of an Embu woman grinding corn at home. The reality is that such women cannot afford to buy the cornmeal being produced by the gigantic machines that have replaced the indigenous practices of food production, as stated earlier.[5] How do neocolonial systems, structures, and discourses produce symbols of reality? What are the implications of the constructions and reconstructions involved in the portrayal of African women? What consumers are permitted to see are merely depoliticized images of women.

Africa is a vast continent comprising countries that have achieved cessation of ethnic rivalries and others that have yet to embrace ethnic unification and successful social and monetary policies. It is a continent where, in spite its natural resources and great potential, many countries have yet to harness the resources for the betterment of their citizens. That poverty and famine exist is undeniable. But the generally unseen face of Africa consists of countries marked by significant economic advances underpinned by a growing and prosperous middle class. It is rare to see these positive aspects of Africa reflected in Western media, which seems to salivate in presenting images of crises, graphic in their visual packaging, with the camera eagerly portraying civil violence and starving, suffering, dying, or dead women and children. The 155 women who participated in my research looked well fed and different from the portrayals in the Western media. Lawyers, doctors, judges, educators, businessmen and women, engineers, and the simple hardworking citizens simply do not exist for many Western media. The camera that is wielded as an instrument of political and cultural manipulation is not used to capture this other face of Africa. The Western propensity to ignore African successes in favour, almost obsessively, of African catastrophe helps us consider how social constructions and reconstructions inform our understanding of representation and portrayal. And the lens through which Westerners view Africa in general, and African women and children in particular, offers distorted images that are blurred by colonial legacies, patriarchy, economic imbalances, and specific political agendas.

Ivan Van Sertima, in *Black Women in Antiquity* (1984), writes that there is a need for African peoples to unearth the knowledges buried beneath the weight of years of oppression under colonial and neocolonial rule. We must acknowledge, revisit, and respect the many sites of ancestral knowledges in order to correct the distorted imaging, identities, and histories of African women. Many of these women, such as the "Candace Queens," were fierce warriors. During the Meroitic period in the kingdom of Kush (today Ethiopia) women were at the forefront of state decisions. As independent rulers, four of these queens, Amanerinas, Amanishakhete, Nawidemak, and Maleqerabar, became "Candaces" – a term derived from the Meroitic *ktke* or *kdke*, which means "queen mother." (Van Sertima 1984). Reclaiming the history and historically denied values and world views of indigenous knowledges as alternative or complementary frameworks of contemporary knowledge production is the first step towards achieving true and valid knowledge. To collect and piece together the shards of African history is to recapture and legitimize a form of technology that is embedded in the cultural psychology and psycho-ecology of a community. It is not enough to identify its technical contents. One must comprehend the beliefs, values, symbols, myths, and social-cultural-cosmological components with which it is associated. In some instances, aspects of these cultures are appropriated without acknowledgment, through either written texts or media, and in the process their authentic derivations are subsumed or obliterated.

Loss of diversity is the price paid for the patriarchal model of progress that pushes inexorably towards monocultures, uniformity, and homogeneity. The invisibility of women's work and knowledges arises from a gender bias, a blind spot in a realistic assessment of women's contributions. It is also rooted in the sectoral, fragmented, and reductionist approach to development that treats forests, livestock, and crops as independent of each other. Women's knowledges are not considered important in a dominant scientific discourse, yet these knowledges are the key to sustainability. Why has the world finally realized that some indigenous communities might hold the answers that could save a planet in peril? Why is indigenous women's expertise not sought in spite of the fact that their unique work and knowledges in biodiversity are found in the interstices of "sectors" and the invisible ecological flows between sectors?

It is through the interface of women and their knowledge of the environment that ecological stability, sustainability, and productivity under resource-scarce conditions are maintained. For example, when agricultural workers come and declare that maize must be planted on its own as a monocrop, on whose knowledge do they rely? In most instances these extension workers do not know that women are extremely environmentally conscious. They are not aware that these women were environmentalists, energy conservationists, and agriculturists long before they could talk. For instance, planting is neither random nor intended only to fill available space; intercropping is a way of eliminating insect damage, sustaining forests, preventing soil erosion, and adding nutrients to the soil. This is critical because it represents a multipurpose support system, in the form of building materials and medicinal plants, for example. Thus, the space is used according to sustainability. By weeding or thinning a maize plantation, rather than random crop cutting, women have learned to examine and then carefully uproot what is not needed. The uprooted plants are then used to create corn mulch, and cows are fed the residue. The women do not need to be told the philosophy behind environmental sustainability, intercropping, thinning, or weeding.

Sittirak (2003, 125) expresses the situation concisely: "Inquiring into my mother's life helped me make critical connections between the theoretical and practical issues related to the environment and development ... My mother doesn't speak the jargon that has become popular in everyday life ... She doesn't busy herself filling blue boxes or wearing a Reduce-Reuse-Recycle button, for she has been doing it all her life for over seventy-five years ... She refuses the unhealthy consumerist lifestyle and has been, and continues to be, a simple and humble environmentalist. Instead of aluminium foil or plastic wrap, my mother uses banana leaves." Sittirak then asks why her mother's voice remains unheard. Why do few people listen to her and why are her perspectives and life stories excluded from formal education and development discourse? Simply put, the answer lies in the Western knowledge producers' reluctance and adamant refusal to acknowledge that indigenous women are reservoirs of information with abilities and knowledge gained over generations of experience. Either something works or it does not. Equally, what cannot be ignored is a prevailing gender bias shared by Western "experts." Among Embu women, knowledge of the land is unquestionable. When a woman is preparing a piece of land for planting, she does not have a manual that outlines the sequences of activities. She knows which weeds to remove in order to prevent their germination, which plants to uproot, which plants will rot, and which will fertilize the soil. When it comes to taking care of the land, an Embu woman knows which plants to keep together so that one will sustain the other. She knows that the scent of onions will drive away the worms that would otherwise attack green peppers; onions are planted with green beans for a similar reason. In the same way, coriander and lemongrass leaves create a scent that serves as a natural pesticide when their plants border the crops. She knows that planting Jerusalem and Sodom's apples around the farm will keep snakes away. She knows that corn silk is highly medicinal and, when boiled, can cure certain illnesses. When corn is harvested, every bit of it is used; the cob is kept and dried for firewood or chopped up and fed to the cows. She knows that maize loosens and oxygenates the soil, and which kinds of beans will hold the soil together and which types loosen it. The knowledges of these women are extraordinary, and their essential and beneficial impact on the lives and livelihood of their families and their communities should not be underestimated, dismissed, or disrespected.

The reality of African women's lives today, and indeed of the African continent and its diverse peoples, cultures, and traditions, generates not only concerns but also controversies. These concerns must be addressed. Some controversies seem to relate more to European and American biases than to facts. The women's voices in this book show the central role played by women and their reverence and understanding of nature, an aspect long recognized within indigenous societies. Forces beyond women's control have severed this connection. As noted earlier, most participants felt that "so much has changed, so much has been destroyed, and there is so much that is foreign" that they have to attentively guide what is left.

Notes

Introduction

1 I thought that Ngugi Wa Thiongo, who began in the 1970s to decry the "colonial mentality" and to promote the virtues of writing in African languages, was a whining, troublesome English professor. I took it for granted that English was one of the languages of Africa because it was, along with Swahili, an official language in my country. People who spoke English were and are considered educated. I never imagined that anyone would tell me, or I would come to the realization, that the English language and the foreign education were a form of colonization and that the beliefs inculcated in me were not really mine – that all the people and cultural symbols I was celebrating were simply not mine. In this blissful ignorance it did not occur to me to question even the most obvious assumptions implicit in my education, for example, that the written word was valued over indigenous knowledges, and why nothing was Kenyan, and African histories were absent in the curriculum.

2 Smith (2001) writes that "globalization of knowledge and Western culture constantly reaffirms the West's view of itself as the centre of legitimate knowledge, the arbiters of what counts as knowledge and the source of 'civilized' knowledge. This form of global knowledge is generally referred to as 'universal' knowledge, available to all and not really 'owned' by anyone, that is, until non-Western scholars make claims to it. When claims like that are made, history is revised (again) so that the story of civilization remains the story of the West. For this purpose, the Mediterranean world, the basin of Arabic culture, and the lands east of Constantinople are conveniently appropriated as part of the story of Western civilization, Western philosophy and Western knowledge. Through imperialism,

however, these cultures, people, and their nation states were repositioned as 'oriental' or 'outsider' in order to legitimate the imposition of colonial rule. For indigenous people from other places, the real lesson to be learned is that we have no claim whatsoever to civilization. It is something which has been introduced from the West, by the West, to indigenous peoples, for our benefit and for which we should be duly grateful."

1. Food Processing

1 Interview with Kanini, 1993; Nathani (1996, 200).
2 Wane (2002).

2. Kenya

1 It is important to point out that this is no longer a common practice, owing to the socio-economic as well as political changes that have taken place over the last few years. However, the practice remains common in places where people feel secure enough to sit outside their houses after dark. Changes in social structure, the loss of close-knit kinship relations, and the lack of means to satisfy basic needs have caused people to give up some of the indigenous social practices. The incidence of assaults, break-ins, and thuggery is high compared to their occurrence two decades ago.
2 A permanent house as pertains herein is one constructed from stones, tiles, or corrugated iron sheets and having a concrete floor.
3 See the work of Amadiume (1998) among the Nbobi people of Nigeria; Presley (1992); and the work of Muthoni Likimani who has documented the role of women during the Mau Mau rebellion.
4 Subordination of women in indigenous society is a new ideology, especially when viewed from a Eurocentric perspective. The dichotomy between men and women in an indigenous setting was not an issue for debate or argument. The indigenous social structure had built-in measures to counteract any inequality experienced by a member of the society. There were laid-out channels for complaints and presentation of grievances, and indigenous "law" courts. Some members of the elite dispute the indigenous practices and see them as ways to control women and subordinate their role in society. They fail to see the context in which these practices were instituted. The rites of passage gave a woman or a man the "entry code" to the next stage in life. For further reading, see Kenyatta (1965).
5 Ahlberg (1991).

6 Dobson (1954).
7 Rodney (1982).
8 Nzomo (1993).
9 Mbilinyi (1994).
10 Ibid.
11 Kiteme (1992).

3. The Everyday Experiences of Embu Women

1 I participated in harvesting, threshing, and winnowing. By the end of the day I had blisters on my palms and my whole body ached. I spilled half of the food crop when winnowing. The women laughed at me and concluded that formal education made a woman "lazy" and took away from her stamina to "be a woman."
2 Charcoal was used when the women had visitors from Nairobi or when household chores preventing them from going out to look for firewood. Out of 177 respondents, 17 women between 60 and 80 years of age used cow dung in addition to firewood for cooking. Most of these women said that firewood had become very scarce, and they preferred to go to the cowshed and collect dry cow dung for cooking purposes. On average, it took 75 per cent (132) of the women between two and three hours each day to collect firewood. Only 4 per cent (7) of the women took between one and two hours, and the rest, 21 per cent (38) of the women, took more than five hours to collect firewood.
3 None of the women who were interviewed wore a watch, but they knew when it was 1:00 p.m., 4:00 p.m., and 10:00 p.m. At 1:00 p.m. the children came home from school for their lunch, and at 4:00 p.m. they came home after the end of their school day. For women whose homes had radios, the last radio broadcast ended at 10:00 p.m. These particular times became significant not only for the women but for the whole community.

6. Indigenous Technology and the Influence of New Innovations

1 V. Shiva (1989).
2 Going to the river is a ritual. I remember that, when I was growing up, washing dirty clothes or going to shower in the river was a community affair. There were certain days of the week – usually Saturdays – when most women from my village would take their clothes to the river. Then there were those days when certain age groups would go to the river for

their monthly or weekly bath. These were socializing events at which women would exchange news.
3. Three stones of approximately one foot in diameter are placed in a triangle. The fire is built in the centre of the triangle and is constantly fed by inserting firewood between the stones. A cooking pot is placed directly above the centre of the triangle, and food for roasting is placed between two of the stones.
4. Trenches are dug according to the size of the width of the cooking pot. A fire is made on the bottom of the trench and is constantly fed with firewood from both sides.

7. Removing the Margins

1. It has often been argued that the name *Kenya* came about because the first European who visited Kenya did not know how to pronounce the name of Mount Kenya, which has a snow-covered peak.
2. When Cucu said that the Europeans ate fire, she was referring to smoking. During her younger years people used to chew tobacco, and smoking was a new phenomenon. The clothes she is referring to are the Western clothes. Kenyans used to wear skins or Indian *Kikoi* (material used as wrap-around) that had come with the traders from the east during the reign of Oman along the east coast.
3. In 2004 I went back to visit the women who were part of my research project. Although many of them have now passed away, what I have done for the community is to establish a community-based organization that looks after forty-five HIV/AIDS orphans, with an emphasis on education.
4. See Ahmadu (1995).
5. Republic of Kenya: Development Plan, 1984–1988.
6. UNICEF/Kenya Central Bureau of Statistics, 1984.

8. Contesting Knowledge

1. Dei (2000a).
2. This is crucial to understanding African indigenous knowledges. Molefi Kete Asante (2000, 1–2) states the concept clearly: "To understand African ways of thinking it is necessary to suspend for a while linearity and to consider the entire world, even the universe or universes as one large system where everything is connected and interconnected. This is the principal view of reality ... Africa is a multi-plex of cultures. This does not mean that the underlying values of the various cultures are significantly

different, as some have tried to contend. Everywhere in Africa there seems to be, from the earliest times, a commonality in the ways humans have approached the universe, environment, society, and the divine."
3 Dei (2000b).
4 Ibid.
5 Wane (2006).

References

Adjei, P.B. 2007. "Decolonising Knowledge Production: The Pedagogic Relevance of Gandhian Satyagraha to Schooling and Education in Ghana." *Canadian Journal of Education* 30 (4): 1046–67. http://dx.doi.org/10.2307/20466678.

Ahlberg, M.B. 1991. *Women, Sexuality and the Changing Social Order: The Impact of Government Politics on Reproductive Behaviour in Kenya*. Philadelphia: Gordon and Breach Science Publishers.

Ahmadu, F. 1995. "Rites and Wrongs." *Pride*, April/May, 43–6.

Aidoo, A.A. 1965. *The Dilemma of a Ghost*. Harlow, UK: Longman Group, Burnt Mill.

Aidoo, A.A. 1998. "The African Woman Today." In *Sisterhood: Feminisms and Power; From Africa to the Diaspora*, ed. O. Nnaemeka, 39–50. Trenton, NJ: Africa World Press.

Alexander, J. 2005. *Pedagogies of Crossing: Meditations of Feminism, Sexual Politics, Memory, and the Sacred*. Durham, NC: Duke University Press.

Amadiume, I. 1998. "Religion, Sexuality and Women's Empowerment in Nwapa's *The Lake Goddess*." In *Emerging Perspectives on Flora Nwapa: Critical and Theoretical Essays*, ed. Marie Umeh, 515–29. Africa World Press.

Asante, M. 2000. *The Painful Demise of Euroentrism: An Afrocentric Response to Critics*. Trenton, NJ: African World Press.

Battiste, M., and J. (Sa'ke'j) Youngblood Henderson, eds. 2000. *Protecting Indigenous Knowledge and Heritage: A Global Challenge*. Saskatoon: Purich Publishing.

Bishop, R. 1998. "Student Centred Learning: Educational Practice That Addresses Cultural Diversity. Published keynote address. Hamilton, Waikato: Distance Education Association of New Zealand.

Blake, C. 1993. "Towards a New Partnership between African Men and Women: The Imperatives of the Development Problematique." Paper presented at the National Women's Conference, Nyeri, Kenya, June 11, 1993.

Boxall, R. 1989. "Storing Grain in the Farm." In *Women and the Food Cycle*, ed. M. Carr, 27–35. London: Intermediate Technology Publications.

Breen, R.M. 1976. "The Politics of Land: The Kenya Land Commission (1932–33) and Its Effects on Land Policy in Kenya." PhD diss., Michigan State University, Department of History.

Cashman, K. 1991. "Systems of Knowledge as Systems of Domination: The Limitations of Established Meaning." *Agriculture and Human Values* 8 (1–2): 49–58. http://dx.doi.org/10.1007/BF01579656.

Charles, N., and M. Kerr. 1988. *Women, Food and Families*. Manchester, UK: Manchester University Press.

Cruikshank, J. 1992. "Oral Traditions and Material Culture: Multiplying Meanings of 'Words' and 'Things.'" *Anthropology Today* 8 (3): 5–9. http://dx.doi.org/10.2307/2783581

Davidson, Basil. 1987. Preface in *Facing Mount Kenya: The Traditional Life of the Gikuyu*, by J. Kenyatta. London: Biddles, 1965.

Dei, G.J.S. 1994. "Afrocentricity: A Cornerstone of Pedagogy. *Anthropology and Education Quarterly* 25 (1): 3–28.

Dei, G.J.S. 2000a. "Rethinking the Role of Indigenous Knowledges in the Academy." *International Journal of Inclusive Education* 4(2), 111–32.

Dei, G.J.S. 2000b. "African Development: The Relevance and Implication of Indigenousness." In *Indigenous Knowledges in Global Contexts: Multiple Readings of Our World*, ed. G. Dei, B. Hall, and D. Rosenberg, 95–108. Toronto: University of Toronto Press.

Dei, G.J.S. 2004. *Schooling and Education in Africa: The Case of Ghana*. Trenton, NJ: Africa World Press.

Dei, G.J.S., and A. Asgharzadesh. 2001. "The Power of Social Theory: The Anti-colonial Discursive Framework." *Journal of Educational Thought* 35 (3): 297–323.

Dei, G.J.S., and S. Doyle-Wood. 2006. "Is We Who Haffi Ride Di Staam: Critical Knowledge/Multiple Knowings: Possibilities, Challenges, and Resistance in Curriculum/Cultural Contexts." In *Curriculum as Cultural Practice: Postcolonial Imaginations*, ed. Y. Kanu, 151–80. Toronto: University of Toronto Press.

Dei, G., B.H. Hall, and D.G. Rosenberg. 2000. *Indigenous Knowledges in Global Contexts: Multiple Readings of Our World*. Toronto: University of Toronto Press.

Delegorgue, A. 1990. *Travels in Southern Africa*. Vol. 1, trans. by Fleur Webb. Pietermaritzburg: University of Natal Press (Killie Campbell Africana Library).

Dobson, B. 1954. "Women's Place in East Africa." *Corona* 6 (12), 454–7.

Einstein, A. 1951. "Why Socialism?" *Monthly Review*.

Elphick, R., and R. Shell. 1989. "Intergroup Relations: Khoikhoi, Settlers, Slaves and Free Blacks, 1652–1795." In *The Shaping of South African Society, 1652–1840*, ed. R. Elphick and H. Giliomee, 184–242. Capetown: Maskew Miller Longman.

Emecheta, B. 1988. "Feminism with a Small 'f.'" In *Criticism and Ideology*, ed. K. Holst Peterson, 173–85. Upsalla, Sweden: Scandinavian Institute of African Studies.

Engels, F.M. 1973. "Function of Golgi Vesicles in Relation to Cell Wall Synthesis in Germinating Petunia Pollen. I. Isolation of Golgi Vesicles." *Acta. Bot. Neerl.* 22:6–13.

Goodleaf, D. 1993. "Under Military Occupation: Indigenous Women, State Violence and Community Resistance." In *And Still We Rise: Feminist Political Mobilizing in Contemporary Canada*, ed. L. Carty, 225–42. Toronto: Women's Press.

Hansen, K.T. 1992. *African Encounters with Domesticity*. Rutgers University Press.

House-Midamba, B. 1990. *Class Development and Gender Inequality in Kenya: 1963–1990*. African Studies, Vol. 20. New York. Edwin Mellen Press.

Ibrahim, M., F. Ibrahim, and C. Slot. 1989. "Assessment of Female Attitudes towards Fuelwood Consumption and Forestry Development." *AHFAD Journal: Women & Change* 6 (1): 3–9.

Ikara, G.K. 1989. "The Economy of Kenya." In *Kenya at a Glance*, ed. S.J.W. Masundu. Nairobi: Color Print Press.

Imam, Ayesha M. 1997. "Engendering African Social Science: An Introductory Essay." In *Engendering African Social Sciences*, ed. Ayesha M. Imam and Amina Mama. Dakar, Senegal: CODESRIA.

James, J. 1993. "African Philosophy, Theory, and 'Living Thinkers.'" In *Spirit, Space and Survival: African American Women in (White) Academe*, ed. J. James and R. Farmer, 31–46. New York: Routledge.

Johnson-Odim, C. 1991. "Common Themes: Different Contexts." In *Third World Women and Feminism*. In *Third World Women and the Politics of Feminism*, ed. C.T. Monhanty, A. Russo, and L. Rorres. Bloomington and Indianapolis: Indiana University Press.

Kabeer, N. 1991. "Rethinking Development from a Gender Perspective: Some Insights from the Decade." Paper presented at the Conference in Southern Africa, University of Natal, Durban.

Kenya, Republic of. 1992. *Annual Agriculture Report*. Nairobi: Government Printer.

References

Kenya Development Plan. 1994–2015. Yearly reports. Nairobi: Government Printers.

Kenya National Bureau of Statistics. 2010. *Kenya Demographic and Health Survey, 2008–09*. Nairobi: Kenya National Bureau of Statistics.

Kenyatta, J. 1965. *Facing Mount Kenya: The Traditional Life of the Gikuyu*. London: Biddles.

Kipusi, N. , and K. Riid, eds. 1992. *To Be a Woman: Video Resource Guide*. Toronto: Inter-church Coalition on Africa.

Kiteme, K. 1992. "The Socioeconomic Impact of the African Market Women Trade in Rural Kenya." *Journal of Black Studies* (Sage Periodicals Press), Sept.

Labai, B. 1992. "Women and Technological Innovations: The Case of Traditional Salt Processing in Sierra Leone." *AHFAD Journal: Women & Change 9* (1): 28–54.

Maina, N., and E.C. Murray. 1993. "Women's Knowledge about Foods: A Kenyan Case Study." A paper presented to Canadian Association of African Studies Conference, 12–15 May, University of Toronto.

Maison, K.B. 2007. "The Indigenous African and Contemporary Education in Ghana: The Challenge of the 21st Century." In *Challenge of Education in Ghana in the 21st Century*, ed. D.E.K. Amenumey, 27–45. Accra, Ghana: Woeli.

Mandala, E.C. 2005. "The Daily Meal." In *The End of Chidyerano: A History of Food and Everyday Life in Malawi, 1800–2004*, 203–38. Portsmouth, NH: Heinemann.

Marx, K. 1997. *Writings of the Young Marx on Philosophy and Society*. Trans. and ed. D. Easton and K.H. Guddat. Indianapolis: Hackett Publishing.

Maundu, P.M., G.W. Ngugi, and C.H.S. Kabuye. 1999. *Traditional Food Plants in Kenya*. Nairobi: Kenya Resource Centre for Indigenous Knowledge, National Museums of Kenya.

Mbilinyi , M., ed. 1994. *Gender Profile in Tanzania*. Dar es Salaam, Tanzania: Tanzania Gender Networking Programme.

Mbilinyi, M. 1997. "Beyond Oppression and Crisis: A Gendered Analysis of Agrarian Structure and Change." In *Engendering African Social Sciences*, ed. Ayesha M. Imam and Amina Mama. Dakar, Senegal: CODESRIA.

Mbithi, M.L. 2012. "Regional Integration and Human Development: Opportunities and Challenges Ahead: The Case of Kenya in EAC." PhD diss., University of Nairobi.

Mburugy, E.K., and F. Ojany. 1989. "The Land and the People." In *Kenya at a Glance*, ed. S.J.W. Musandu. Nairobi: Color Print Ltd.

Meden, Von der, M., and K. Meyers. 1986. "The Hidden Talent: Women Creators and Inventors." *Women's International Cross-Cultural Exchange* (10).

Mies, M. 1986. *Indian Woman in Subsistence and Agricultural Labour*. Geneva: Place.
Miller, R. 1999. "Holistic Education and the Emerging Culture." Transcripts.
Momsen, J.H. 1991. *Women and Development in the Third World*. London: Routledge.
Nasimiyu, R. 1997. "Changing Women's Rights over Property in Western Kenya." In *African Families and the Crisis of Social Change*, ed. T.S. Weisner, C. Bradley, and P.L. Kilbride, 283–98. Westport, CT: Bergin and Garvey.
Nathani, C.N. 1996. "Sustainable Development: Indigenous Forms of Food Processing Technologies; A Kenyan Case Study." PhD. diss., University of Toronto.
Nfah-Abbenyi, J.M. 1997. *Gender in African Women's Writing: Identity, Sexuality, and Difference*. Indiana University Press.
Nnaemeka, O. 1997. Introduction to *Sisterhood, Feminisms and Power: From Africa to Diaspora*, ed. O. Nnaemeka, 1–35. Asmara, Eritrea: Africa World Press.
Nyamnjoh, F.B. 2004. "A Relevant Education for African Development: Some Epistemological Considerations." *Africa Development / Afrique et Developpement* (Council for the Development of Social Science Research in Africa) XXIX (1): 161–84.
Nzomo, M. 1987. "Women, Democracy and Development." In *Democracy Theory and Practice in Africa*, ed. O. Oyugi and A. Gitonga, 111–13. Nairobi: Heinemann.
Nzomo, M. 1993. "Women, Democracy and Development." In *Democracy, Theory, and Practice in Africa*, ed. O. Oyugi and A. Gitonga, 111–31. Nairobi: Heinemann.
Ogundipe-Leslie, M. 1994. "African Women, Culture, and Another Development." In Recreating Ourselves: African Women and Critical Transformations, 21–42. Trenton, NJ: Africa World Press.
p'Bitek, O. 1995. *Song of Lawino*. Vol. 2. East African Publishers.
Peters, R.S. 1966. "The Philosophy of Education." In *The Study of Education*, ed. J.W. Tibble. London: Routledge and Kegan Paul.
Presley, C.A. 1992. *Kikuyu Women, the Mau Mau Rebellion, and Social Change in Kenya*. Boulder, CO: Westview Press.
Rodney, W. 1982. *How Europe Underdeveloped Africa*. Washington, DC: Howard University Press.
Salim, I., and K. Janmohamed. 1989. "Historical Development." In *Kenya at a Glance*, ed. S.J.W. Musandu. Nairobi: Colour Print Ltd.
Seabrook, J. 1993. "The Metamorphoses of Colonialism." *Just World Trust (JUST)*, 21.

Semali, L., and J.L. Kincheloe. 1999. *What Is Indigenous Knowledge? Voices from the Academy.* New York: Falmer Press.

Sen, G. 1985. "Women Agricultural Labourers: Regional Variations in Incidence and Employment." In *Tyranny and Household*, ed. N. Banerjee and D. Jain, 124–45. New Delhi: Vikas Publishers.

Shahjahan, R. 2007. *The Everyday as Sacred: Trailing Back by the Spiritual Proof Fence in the Academy.* PhD diss., Department of Theory and Policy Studies in Education, Ontario Institute for Studies in Education of the University of Toronto.

Shiva, V. 1989. *Staying Alive: Women, Ecology, and Development.* London: Zed Books.

Shiva, V. 2000. *Stolen Harvest: The Hijacking of Global Food Supply.* Cambridge, MA: South End Press.

Sifuna, D.1992. *Development of Education in Africa: The Kenyan Experience.* Nairobi: Kenya Initiative.

Simwogere, E. 1992. "Cassava Processing and Utilization in Luwero, Uganda." *AHFAD Journal: Women & Change* 9 (1).

Sittirak, S. 2003. *The Daughters of Development: Women in a Changing Environment.* Spinifex Press.

Smith, L.T. 1999. *Decolonizing Methodologies: Research and Indigenous Peoples.* London: Zed Books.

Somé, M.P. 1994. *Of Water and the Spirit: Ritual Magic and Imitation in the Life of an African Shaman.* New York: Tarcher/Putnam.

Sorrenson, M.P.K. 1968. *Origins of European Settlement in Kenya.* Vol. 2. Oxford University Press.

Stamp, P. 1992. *Technology, Gender, and Power in Africa.* Ottawa: IDRC.

Steady, F.C. 1989. "African Feminism: A Worldwide Perspective." In *Women in Africa and the African Diaspora*, ed. R. Terborg-Penn, 3–24. Boston: Harvard University Press.

Thiong'o, N.W. 1985. "The Language of African Literature." *New Left Review* 150 (March/April): 109–27.

Thiong'o, N.W. 1986: *Decolonizing the Mind: The Politics of Language in African Literature.* Nairobi: East African Publishing.

Thiong'o, N.W. 2005. *Petals of Blood.* London: Penguin Classics.

Van Sertima, I.V. 1984. *Black Women in Antiquity.* New Brunswick, NY: Transaction Books.

Wane, N.N. 2002. "African Women's Technologies: Applauding the Self, Reclaiming Indigenous Space." *Postcolonial Journal of Education* 1 (1): 45–66.

Wane, N.N. 2003a. "Educating the Other: Taking Charge of Their Dreams": A Review of Four Books: Ladson-Billings; Henry; Valenzuela; Morris and Morris. *Curriculum Inquiry* 33 (3): 321–30.

Wane, N.N. 2003b. "Embu Women: Food Production and Traditional Knowledges." *Resources for Feminist Research Journal* 30 (1 and 2), Spring/Summer.

Wane, N.N. 2005. "African Indigenous Knowledge: Claiming, Writing, Storing, Sharing the Discourse." *Journal of Thought*, 40 (2): 27–46.

Wane, N.N. 2006. *Is Decolonization Possible?* In *Anti-colonialism and Education: The Politics of Resistance*, ed. G.J.S. Dei and A. Kempf, 87–107). Rotterdam: Sense Publishers.

Wane, N.N., and W.T. Gathenya. 2003. "The Yokes of Gender and Class: The Policy Reforms and Implications for Equitable Access to Education in Kenya." *Managing Global Transitions* 1 (2): 169–94.

Waring, M. 1999. *Counting for Nothing: What Men Value and What Women Are Worth*. Toronto: University of Toronto Press

Wekiya, I. 1992. "Shea Butter Extraction in Ghana." *AHFAD Journal* 9 (1): 17–27.

Wint-Bauer, V. 1986. "Women and Food Processing in Guyana." *Women's World*.

Wolff, Richard D. 1974. *Economics of Colonialism: Britain and Kenya, 1870–1930*. New Haven, CT: Yale University Press.

Zeleza, T. 1993. "Trial of an Academic Tourist." *CODESRIA Bulletin*, 1.

Zeleza, T. 1997. *Manufacturing African Studies and Crises*. Dakar: Codesria Book Series.

Zeleza, T . 2010. "African Diasporas: Toward a Global History." *African Studies Review* 53 (1).

Index

Aidoo, Ama Ataa, 16, 87–8, 103
Alice, 27–8, 48, 60–1, 74–5, 84, 85–6
Angelina, 27
ashes: as construction material, 35, 36, 49, 60, 69; as preservatives, 64–6, 69, 70, 77

bananas, 45, 48, 50, 77, 105
Battiste, M., 11
beans, 49–51, 53, 64, 76, 106
beer, 25–6, 51, 81–2
Bishop, R., 24
Boxall, R., 63, 64

Cashman, K., 88
cassava, 50, 78
celebrations and rituals: decision making, 72; and food potency, 11; foods, 50, 85, 94; generational differences, 72, 94–5; impact of environmental degradation on, 32; new home ceremony, 36; rites of passage (ear piercing, circumcision), 72, 93–5; use of beer, 36, 51, 72, 85; use of sacrifice, 33. *See also* spirituality
chapatti, 50
children: as ancestor replacements, 34; childlessness, 27–8; chores, 15, 25, 52, 54–5, 62; naming practices, 34. *See also* education; motherhood
Ciarunji, 23, 29, 36, 47, 55, 58, 64, 65, 69, 76–7, 85
circumcision, 72, 94, 95. *See also* celebrations and rituals
climate: drought, 31–3; dry and wet seasons, 59–60; overview, 3–4, 61; unpredictability, 32, 69–70
colonialism: and African feminism, 13–14, 39; discrediting of indigenous knowledge, 9, 99–100; and education, 6–7, 39, 67, 95, 99–101, 107n1; overview, 38–43; pre-colonial systems, 17, 39–40, 79–80, 89–90, 104–5, 108n4; and SAPs, 40–3, 67–8; Victorian values, 38–9, 102–3
cooking. *See* food preparation
cookware: grinding stones, 23–4, 29, 51, 79, 84; mortar and pestle, 29, 51, 79, 84; overview, 21–2, 29, 84; social histories of, 22, 29; utensils and pots, 21–2, 29, 79, 82–4
corn. *See* maize
Counting for Nothing (Waring), 44
cow dung: as construction material, 22, 35, 36, 49, 60, 69–70, 84; for

food preservation, 64–5, 69, 70, 77; for heat, 109n2
crops. *See* food production cycle
Cruikshank, J., 21
Cucu, 20, 32–3, 51, 53, 66, 72–3, 75, 77, 84, 85, 87, 90–1, 110n2 (ch. 7)

daily routines. *See* everyday life of women
decision making, 27, 47, 56, 72–6
Dei, George, 7, 11, 24, 68, 102
demographics: family size, 34, 41; farming decline, 37; food security, 57; health indicators, 96; marriage, 41; maternal deaths, 43; mobility, 36, 37; population, 31, 41; population growth rate, 31, 57; rural *vs.* urban, 31, 41
development programs (SAPs), 40–3, 67–8
digging sticks *vs.* tractors, 23–4, 81, 84, 85

ear piercing, 72, 93–4
economy, household. *See* household economy
economy, Kenya, 36–8
education: benefits of Western education, 7–8; community discipline of children, 94; and gender roles, 39–40, 93; impact of colonialism, 6–7, 39, 67, 95, 99–101; indigenous ways of knowing, 51–2, 91–4; languages, 107n1; literacy, 39, 71; loss of indigenous knowledge, 5, 7, 29–30, 67, 77, 86; overview, 92–3; reforms proposed, 68–9, 77–8, 96–7. *See also* knowledge production
Einstein, Albert, 102

elders: conversation protocols, 90–1; educational role of, 5, 68, 93; research role of, 11. *See also* Ciarunji; Cucu; generational differences; Mama; Rwamba; Wachiuma
electricity, 32, 83
Embu culture: ethnic group, 31; mobility, 36; responsibilities and rights, 14–15, 24–5, 93; roles and customs, 34–6. *See also* celebrations and rituals; everyday life of women; feminism, African; homesteads; indigenous knowledge; knowledge production
Emecheta, Buchi, 14, 15–16
employment of women outside of home, 15, 34, 37–8
energy. *See* electricity; firewood; heat and light
environment: climate unpredictability, 32, 69–70; deforestation, 32, 66, 70, 80; degradation of, 31–5, 86; female indigenous knowledge, 23–4, 32–3, 65–6, 105–6; harm from new technologies, 24–5, 64–7, 69, 71, 77, 84; indigenous world view, 93; land and spirituality, 23–4, 32–3
ethnic groups and languages, 4, 31, 107n1
everyday life of women: and African feminism, 13–18, 40–3; compared with men's lives, 75; crop production, 45–7; decision making, 47, 72; education of children, 25; heavy demands, 60–1; multitasking, 19, 53–5, 90; oral tradition, 17, 20–1, 90–2; power relations, 74–5; schedules, 48, 54–5, 60–1, 75; seasonal activities, 35, 59–60; shared and hired labour, 48–9; time, 25, 52–4,

90–1, 109nn2–3; undervalued, 44–5, 55, 61–2. *See also* firewood; homesteads; household economy; indigenous knowledge; water; *entries beginning with* food

families. *See* children; motherhood
females. *See* women
feminism, African: impact of SAPs on, 40–3; overview, 13–18
fireplaces and stoves, 21–2, 54, 82–3, 110n3 (ch. 6)
firewood: drying, 20; environmental degradation, 31; overview, 58–9, 80, 109n2; in stoves, 54
food: about food dishes, 50–1; cash crops, 45–6, 73, 74–5; ceremonial foods, 85, 94; food security, 31, 73, 78; household crops, 45; impact of new technologies, 4–5, 25–6; nutrition, 51, 76–7; overview, 76–8; serving patterns, 15, 61; shared food, 50; as social power, 55–6, 74–5, 82, 88–9
food and gender: beer production, 81–2; boys' roles, 52; decision making, 56; government policies, 56–8, 61, 86; male construction of indigenous technology, 29, 56, 84; male ownership of cash crops, 45–6, 73, 74–5; pre-colonial systems, 81
food harvesting, preservation, and storage: costs, 5, 49, 64, 65, 77; drying, 20, 50, 63; generational differences, 22, 49, 58, 65–7, 70–1, 95; granaries, 35, 57–8, 83–4; indigenous technologies, 64–6, 69, 70–1, 106; moisture content, 47, 48, 50, 63, 66; new technologies, 49, 64–7,
69, 71, 77; overview, 48–50, 63–5, 69; specific foods, 49–50, 55, 59, 63; storage, 20, 63–4, 69, 84; threshing and winnowing, 48, 49–50, 56; wooden sticks, 49, 79, 84. *See also* food production cycle
food preferences: costs, 86, 103; generational differences, 76, 86; indigenous foods, 25–6, 50–1, 76–7; non-indigenous foods, 50; packaged foods, 23, 76, 86, 103; Western *vs.* indigenous, 23, 51, 76–8, 103
food preparation: costs, 5, 30, 84, 85; education of children, 51–2, 91–2; fireplaces and stoves, 21–2, 54, 82–3, 110n3 (ch. 6); gender and technology ownership, 81; generational differences, 22, 51–2, 85–6; grinding stones, 23–4, 29, 51, 79, 84; indigenous technologies, 21–2, 25, 29, 82–4; mortar and pestle, 29, 51, 79, 84; multitasking, 19, 53–4; new technologies, 21–2, 26, 29, 81–5; seasonal activities, 59–60; spiritual and community aspects, 26, 29, 84–5; time, 53–4, 76, 109n3. *See also* cookware
food production cycle: crop cultivation and rotation, 70; decision making, 47, 56, 73, 75; gender roles, 45, 56, 73; indigenous knowledge, 23, 47–9; intercropping *vs.* mono-cropping, 46–7, 105–6; new grains, 64; overview, 46–9; pre-colonial systems, 81, 89–90; seasonal activities, 47–8, 59–60; spiritual aspects, 84–5; timing of events, 47, 50, 56; tractors *vs.* digging sticks, 23–4, 81, 84, 85;

weeding, 70, 105–6. *See also* food harvesting, preservation, and storage
food security, 31, 56–7, 73, 78
fruit, 46, 50
fuel. *See* firewood; heat and light

gender: African feminism, 13–18, 40–3; cash *vs.* household crops, 45–6, 73; decision making, 56, 72–5; domestic roles, 15, 81; health, 88; impact of SAPs on, 40–3; knowledge validity, 104–5; male ownership, 27; roles and customs, 34–6; women in government, 37–8. *See also* food and gender; patriarchy
generational differences: celebrations, 72; decision making, 75–6; food preferences, 76, 86; food preparation, 22, 51–2, 85–6; food preservation, 22, 49, 58, 65–7, 70, 95; health, 90; marriage, 75–6; responsibilities and rights, 14–15; rituals and ceremonies, 94–5
government of Kenya: gender issues, 37–8, 74; national food policies, 56–8, 61; piped water, 59, 80–2
granaries, 35, 48, 57–8, 83–4
grinding mills, 4–5, 23–4, 81–2
grinding stones, 23–4, 29, 51, 79, 84

harvesting crops. *See* food harvesting, preservation, and storage
health: gender roles, 88; overview, 90, 95–7; of women, 61
heat and light, 21, 83, 109n2. *See also* fireplaces and stoves
Henderson, J. (Sa'ke'j) Youngblood, 11
homesteads: home maintenance, 35, 60; household garden (*shamba*), 23, 49, 75; "kitchen" area, 20–1, 36, 82; overview, 35–6, 108n1; permanent homes, 108n2; semi-permanent homes, 27, 35–6; traditional furnishings, 20
honey, 45
household economy: annual incomes, 28, 29, 41; cash crops, 45–6, 74–5; household crops, 45–6; impact of SAPs on, 40–3; measurements of women's work, 44–5; overview, 10

Imam, Ayesha M., 61
indigenous, as term, 12
indigenous knowledge: and African feminism, 16–18; educational reform to include, 68–9, 77–8, 96–7; embarrassment about, 29, 58, 65–7, 86; impact of SAPs on, 67–8; interconnectedness, 25, 110n2 (ch. 8); overview, 4–5, 10–12, 98–9, 110n2 (ch. 8); pluralist way of knowing, 98–9; pre-colonial systems, 79–80, 89–90, 104–5; validity of, 98–106, 107n2. *See also* food harvesting, preservation, and storage; food preparation; food production cycle
International Monetary Fund (SAPs), 40–3, 67–8

James, Joy, 14

Kabeer, N., 48, 60
Kanini, 22, 46, 48, 60, 61, 73, 83
Kanyiva, 28–9, 48, 53, 54, 86
Kenya: economy, 36–8; ethnic and language groups, 4, 31, 107n1; food shortages, 56–7; geography, 3–4; impact of SAPs on, 40–3; pre-colonial

systems, 39–40, 79–80, 89–90, 104–5. *See also* climate; colonialism; demographics; Embu culture; environment; government of Kenya
Kenyatta, J., 93
Kincheloe, J.L., 99–100
knowledge production: oral tradition, 90–2; overview, 87, 98–9; pluralist way of knowing, 98–9; and power relations, 88–9; threshold crossing, 88, 91; validity of indigenous knowledge, 98–106, 107n2; Western trend to homogeneity, 104–5

lamps and lanterns, 83
land, 31–4. *See also* environment; ownership of resources
languages and ethnic groups, 4, 31, 107n1
latrines, 35, 36
Likimani, Muthoni, 38
literacy, 39, 71
Luyia culture, 89

Maina, N., 88
Maison, K.B., 94, 102
maize, 48, 49, 50, 57, 59, 64, 76, 78, 105
maize grinding mills, 4–5, 8, 23–4
males. *See* men
Mama, 25–6
Mandale, E.C., 4
marigolds, 64–6, 69, 70–1, 77
Marigu, 29, 46–7
marriage: childlessness, 27–8, 34, 74; employment outside home, 34; generational differences, 75–6; geographic separation of spouses, 29, 41, 56; power of food, 15, 82; wedding gifts, 22; wives as property, 61
Mbilinyi, M., 10, 40, 45
Mbithi, M.L., 52
meat, 46, 50
medicine. *See* health
men: domestic roles, 15; everyday life of, 75; fatherhood, 34; financial obligations, 15; home construction, 36; responsibilities and rights, 14–15; roles and customs, 34–6. *See also* gender; marriage; patriarchy
Mies, M., 38
Mill, John Stuart, 68
Miller, R., 24
millet, 48, 49, 78
Momsen, J.H., 60
mortar and pestle, 29, 51, 79, 84
motherhood: child as Creator's gift, 15; childbirth impact on daily life, 47; childlessness, 27–8, 34, 74; demographics, 41, 43; gender roles, 15; overview, 34
Murray, E.C., 88

Nasimiyu, R., 89–90
Ndungu, Njoki, 74
Nfah-Abennyah, J.M., 14, 16–17
Njura, 26, 48, 49, 54, 65, 71
Nnaemeka, O., 14
nutrition, 51, 76–7
Nyamnjoh, F.B., 98
Nzomo, M., 38, 42

Ogundipe-Leslie, M., 14
oral tradition: and education of women, 90–2; knowledge validity, 98–100, 107n2; lullabies, 93–4; overview, 17, 20–1. *See also* indigenous knowledge

ownership of resources: and gender, 39–40, 61, 73–5; impact of colonialism, 39; overview, 73–4; patriarchy, 27; pre-colonial systems, 89–90

patriarchy: cash crops, 45–6, 73, 74–5; domestic life, 15, 61, 75; impact of SAPs on, 40–3; male ownership, 27, 39, 46; overview, 15, 34. *See also* men
p'Bitek, O., 52, 100–1
peas, 49
planting crops. *See* food production cycle
polygamy, 34–5, 73, 74, 82
porridge, 25, 50–1, 55
potatoes, 50, 64, 76, 77
pots, cooking. *See* cookware
preferred foods. *See* food preferences
preparing food. *See* food preparation
preserving food. *See* food harvesting, preservation, and storage

religion, 101. *See also* spirituality
research project: facilitator's role, 3, 5, 8–10, 11; interviews, 3, 6, 11, 72, 90; overview, 3–9; threshold crossing, 5–6, 88, 91; women's voices, 5, 9, 10, 13, 19, 99–100
rice, 50
Rwamba, 24–5, 27, 33–4, 66, 69, 75, 77–8, 81, 84, 87

SAPs (structural adjustment programs), 40–3, 67–8
Seabrook, Jeremy, 67
Semali, L., 99–100
Sen, G., 37, 38
Shiva, V., 26, 70, 80, 99–100
Sittirak, S., 105–6

Smith, L.T., 99
Somé, Malidoma, 7, 11
Song of Lawino (p'Bitek), 52, 100–1
spirituality: the Creator, 15, 33, 72; and environment, 33; and food preparation, 84–5; and indigenous world view, 92–3, 98; and land, 23–4; overview, 24; validity of knowledge, 99–101, 107n2. *See also* celebrations and rituals
Steady, Filomina Chiomia, 14
stoves and fireplaces, 21–2, 54, 82–3, 110n3 (ch. 6)
structural adjustment programs (SAPs), 40–3, 67–8
sugar cane: cash crops, 45–6; and technologies, 25–6, 81–2

teas, 26, 85
terminology, 12
three-stone fireplaces and stoves, 21–2, 54, 82–3, 110n3 (ch. 6)
threshing, 49–50
threshold crossing protocol, 5–6, 88, 91
time: in everyday life, 25, 52–4, 90–1, 109n3; multitasking, 19, 53
To Be a Woman (film), 40
tractors *vs.* digging sticks, 23–4, 81, 84, 85
traditional, as term, 12

utensils, cooking. *See* cookware

Van Sertima, Ivan, 104
vegetables, 45–6, 50–1, 70, 76

Wachiuma, 20–2, 49–50, 69, 70, 73, 79
Waithera, 28–9

Wane, Njoki Nathani, 4–10, 18, 87, 90–1, 107n1, 109n1 (ch. 5), 109n2 (ch. 6), 110n3 (ch. 7)
Wangeci, 28–9, 65, 83, 85
Wanja, 66
Waring, Marilyn, 44–5
Warue, 49, 65–6, 81, 83
water: containers, 20, 22, 58, 83; overview, 58–60, 80–1; piped water, 59, 80–2; rainwater, 35–6, 59; from river, stream, or well, 35, 58–60, 80, 109n2 (ch. 6)
Wawira, 28, 46, 47, 48, 74, 85
weeding, 70, 105–6
Western culture: education in Africa, 7–8; everyday life of women, 103; feminism, 17; homogeneity, 104–5; images of Africa, 10, 103–4; indigenous *vs.* Western food preferences, 51, 76–8, 103; responsibilities and rights, 14–15, 24–5, 93. *See also* colonialism
winnowing, 50
womanism, 14
women: employment outside of home, 26, 34, 37–8; home construction, 36; responsibilities and rights, 14–15. *See also* everyday life of women; gender; marriage; motherhood
World Bank (SAPs), 40–3, 67–8

yams, 45, 78

Zeleza, T., 18, 19, 79